AF711275

Alfred's Basic Chord Approach To

Electronic Keyboards

A BEGINNING METHOD FOR ALL INSTRUMENTS WITH AUTOMATIC RHYTHMS & CHORDS

Lesson Book 1

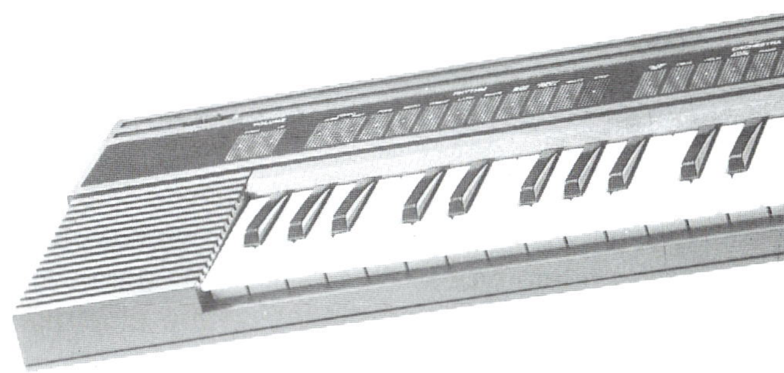

Willard A. Palmer

Thomas Palmer

Morton Manus

Keyboards courtesy of:

BIG VALLEY MUSIC
RESEDA, CALIFORNIA

JOHN WALTRIP'S MUSIC CENTERS
ARCADIA, CALIFORNIA

Foreword

HOW TO USE THIS BOOK

Electronic keyboards with automatic rhythms and chords provide, at low cost, many exciting features that translate into rapid progress, particularly in the earliest stages of music study. In a very short time a beginning student can produce music with melody, harmony and rhythm, using a variety of tonal colors, including piano, organ, orchestral instruments, bells, percussion instruments, etc. Students are thus motivated to practice the same pieces over and over, using the different sounds to make repetition a delight rather than monotony.

These instruments provide a variety of realistic drum sounds that are useful in helping the student to master the intricacies of counting rhythms, reading music, and feeling the inner pulse of the music. Students who do not like to play with a metronome enjoy playing with drum sounds.

There are many ways of combining the electronic keyboard with the acoustic piano at the lesson, and many teachers often use an electronic keyboard to provide drum sounds and chord accompaniments while students play certain types of pieces on the acoustic piano. It is interesting and highly motivating to have the students also play their piano pieces on the electronic keyboard, using some of the many exciting and unique sounds that are available.

ABOUT "SINGLE FINGER" CHORDS & "FINGERED CHORDS"

"Single Finger" chords make it possible for beginners to play professional-sounding left-hand accompaniments with minimum knowledge and effort. Different makes of instruments produce these chords by slightly different means. These various approaches are clearly and simply explained in this book, which may be used with any of the leading brands of electronic keyboards, including YAMAHA, CASIO, TECHNICS, BALDWIN, REALISTIC, LOWRY, the new KAWAI and many others.

All of the above brands also make use of "Fingered Chords," which produce all the automatic rhythm effects, variations, etc., but have an important advantage—they are identically formed on all makes of instruments. The use of fingered chords is emphasized in this book, and these chords are presented in a careful, step-by-step presentation, with keyboard diagrams clearly shown on the pages in which such chords are used. These chords may also be used on the acoustic piano, the organ, the synthesizer or any other keyboard instrument, whether or not the instrument is equipped with automatic chords and rhythms. By using such a presentation, this book serves as a starting point from which a thorough understanding of the basics of music may be built.

A PRACTICAL AND MOTIVATING APPROACH

This book begins by having the student do the simplest things that make the most interesting sounds, while learning to read and play basic rhythms. The automatic features of the instrument are immediately used. Reading music is taught by INTERVAL, rather than by the old-fashioned method of counting up or down on the lines and spaces of the staff.

THE "WAVE OF THE FUTURE"

Electronic keyboards are selling in the millions. They are here to stay, but students who buy these keyboards and attempt to learn to play them without the help of a teacher are not always likely to succeed. These remarkable instruments offer an opportunity for teachers to reach more students than ever before, and to open for them the doors to the wonderful world of music-making.

CONTENTS

Position at the Electronic Keyboard

Metal or wooden stands are available as accessories for many keyboards. These stands hold the instrument in the correct playing position, so the surface of the keys is 27 to 30 inches from the floor.

If you can not obtain a stand for your instrument, a desk or table will do.

Good posture at the keyboard makes playing easier. Sit squarely in front of the keyboard, and observe the following points:

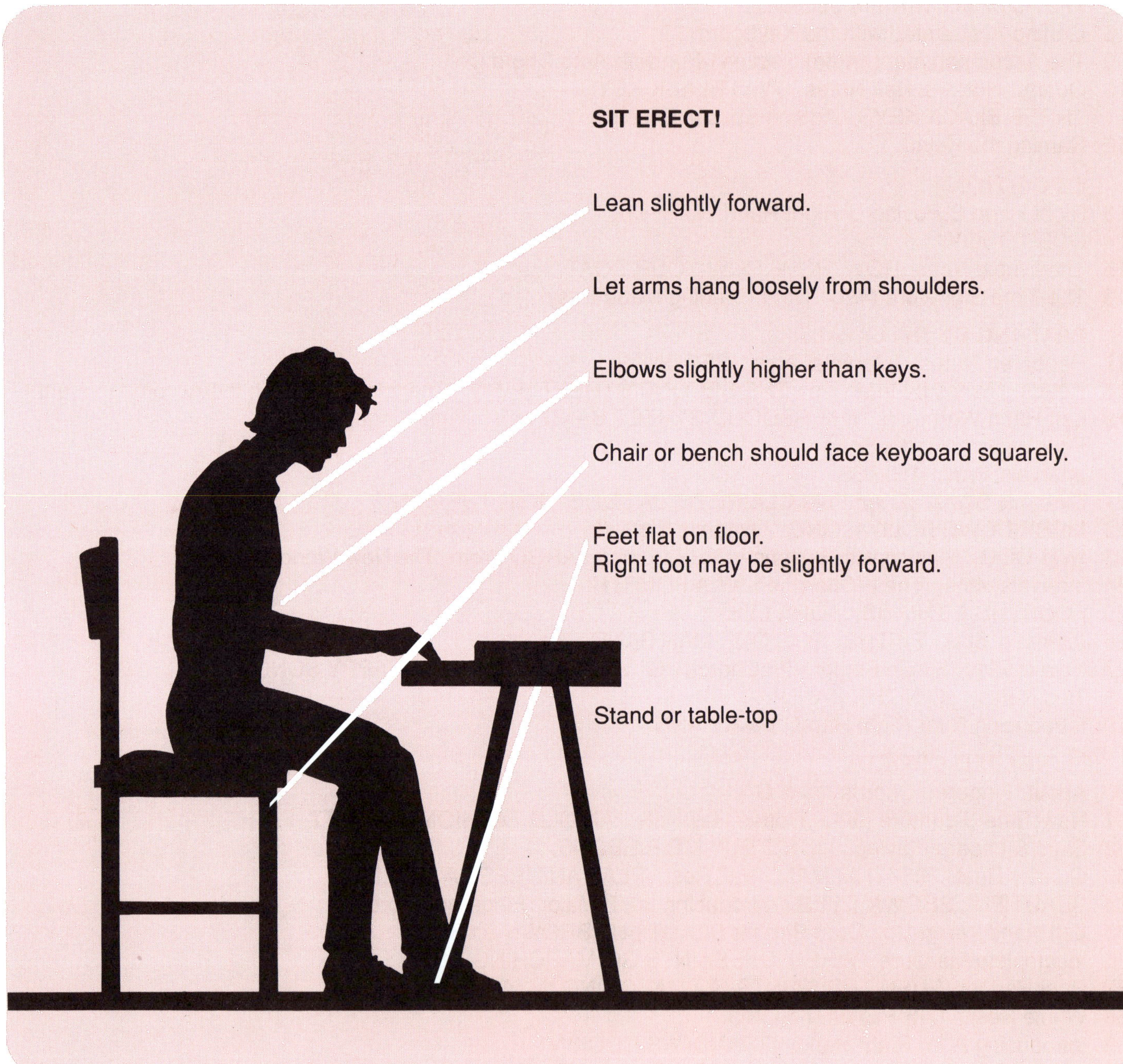

About Music Racks or Holders

Most instruments have a music rack, but a few small table-top instruments do not. You can improvise a holder for your music books by using an easel-type picture frame on the table behind your instrument, or you can tape a piece of heavy cardboard on the back of your instrument, with an easel-type flap attached to hold it at the proper angle.

A free-standing metal music stand may be purchased at your music store.

This book is intended for use with an electronic keyboard that has AUTOMATIC RHYTHMS and CHORDS and 44 or more keys.

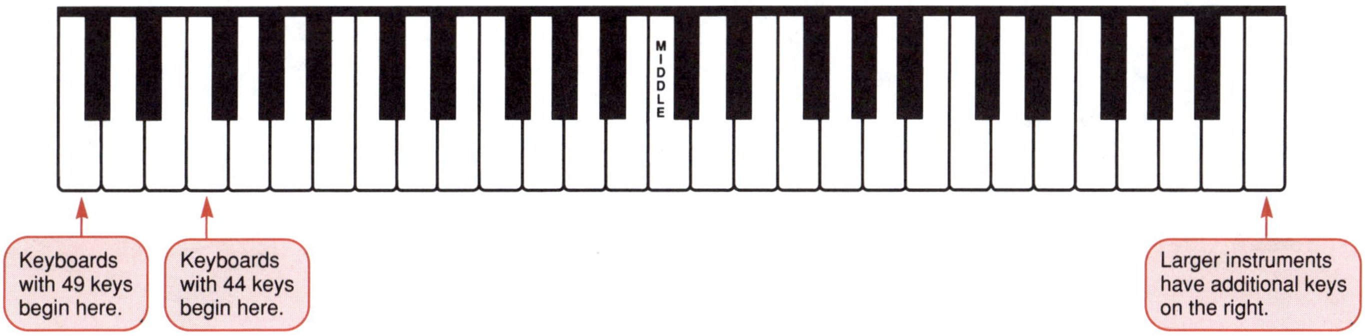

How Fingers Are Numbered

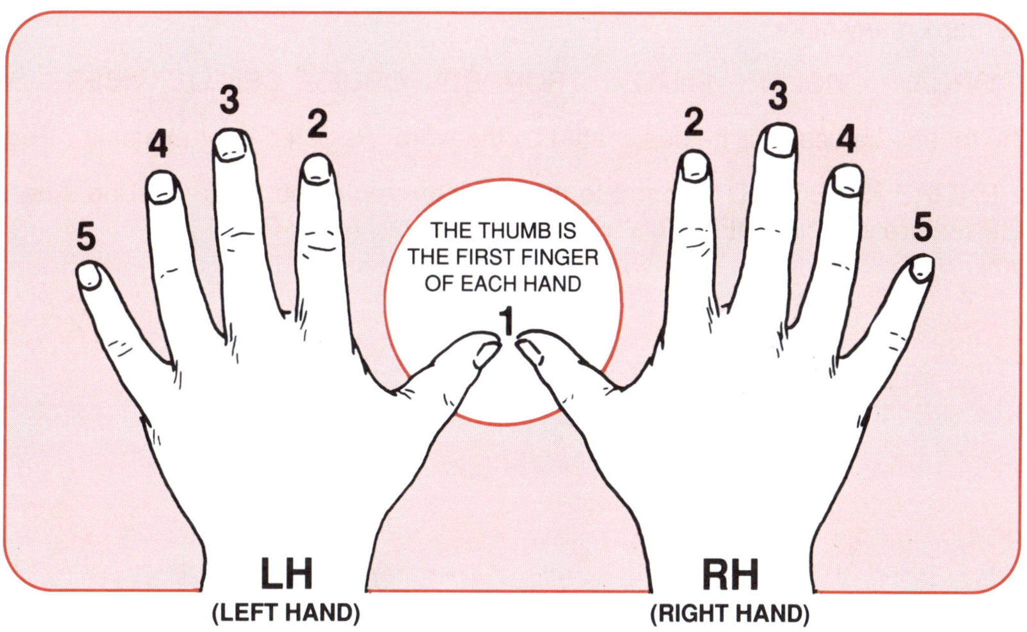

Before you begin to play, practice moving each finger as you say its number aloud.

Curve your fingers, because:

Straight fingers have different lengths!

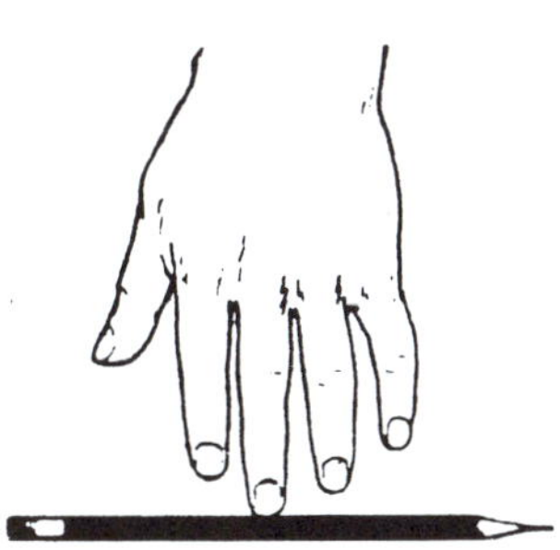

Curved fingers can have the same lengths!

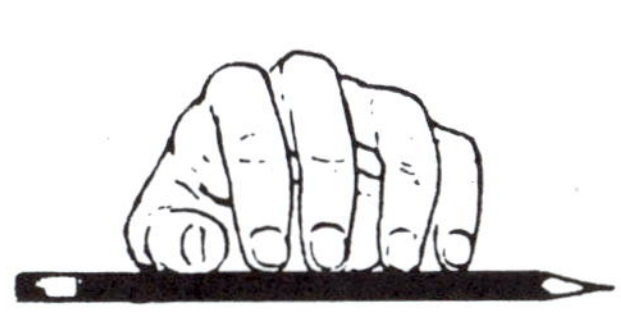

Pretend you have a bubble in your hand. Hold the bubble gently, so it doesn't break!

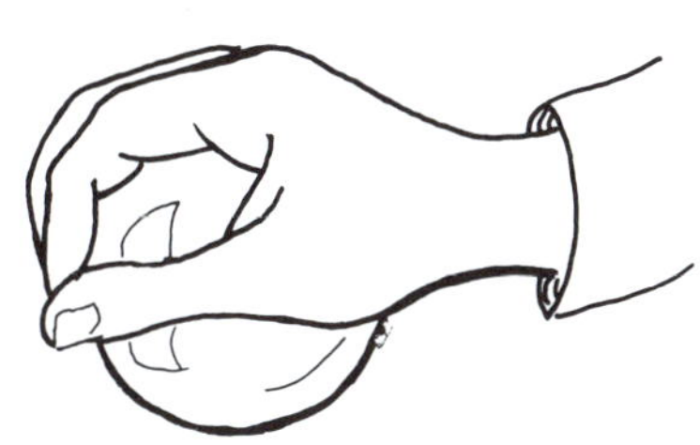

Your Own Orchestra!

With your electronic keyboard, you have an orchestra at your disposal!

In the ORCHESTRA or TONE SELECTION section of your instrument you will find some or all of the following sounds, and perhaps many more:

PIANO ORGAN VIOLIN FLUTE TRUMPET OBOE CELLO VIBES SYNTHE

In this book, the tone to be used will be designated by the word "Register"—for example, "**Register:** PIANO."

To make your ENTIRE KEYBOARD respond to the Register you select, you must be sure the AUTOMATIC (BASS) CHORD feature is turned OFF. This will be indicated by "**Auto:** OFF."

Ready to Begin!

1. Turn POWER ON.
2. Prepare your instrument as follows:
   Auto: OFF **Rhythm:** OFF (Do not press START!) **Register:** PIANO
3. Adjust the MAIN VOLUME about half way.
4. With the 2nd finger of your LH (left hand), play ANY KEY, black or white, on the LEFT half of the keyboard. BE SURE TO CURVE YOUR FINGERS! Play several more keys with the LH.
5. With the 2nd finger of your RH (right hand), play ANY KEY, black or white, on the RIGHT half of the keyboard. Use just enough pressure to make each key go ALL THE WAY DOWN. Play several more keys with the RH.
6. Play more keys, using the 2nd finger of either hand, trying some different Registers. Listen to the different sounds you can create!

The Automatic Rhythm Section

There is a set of drums in your keyboard, ready to automatically provide a variety of professional sounding rhythmic backgrounds for your playing, at any tempo (speed) you choose.

Various makes and models of keyboards offer a dozen or more different rhythms. Some of those most frequently included are:

SWING POP SLOW ROCK COUNTRY ROCK 'N' ROLL MARCH DISCO WALTZ

The RHYTHM SECTION is controlled by START and STOP buttons. On some instruments, this is combined in one START/STOP button.

1. Turn the MASTER or MAIN VOLUME up about half way.

2. Turn the RHYTHM VOLUME up a little.

3. Press the button marked SWING or MARCH. Touch the START button and listen!
   Adjust the volume controls to whatever loudness you prefer.

4. The SPEED of the rhythmic beats is determined by the TEMPO setting.
   Adjust the tempo to moderately slow speed.

5. The slash-marks (/) below are separated into MEASURES by vertical bar-lines. TAP or CLAP along with the main beats of the rhythm, ONCE for each slash-mark (FOUR times for each measure). Count "1-2-3-4" as you tap or clap each measure. This will be just like clapping along with a popular song. If you need assistance, your teacher will show you how to "feel" the rhythm.

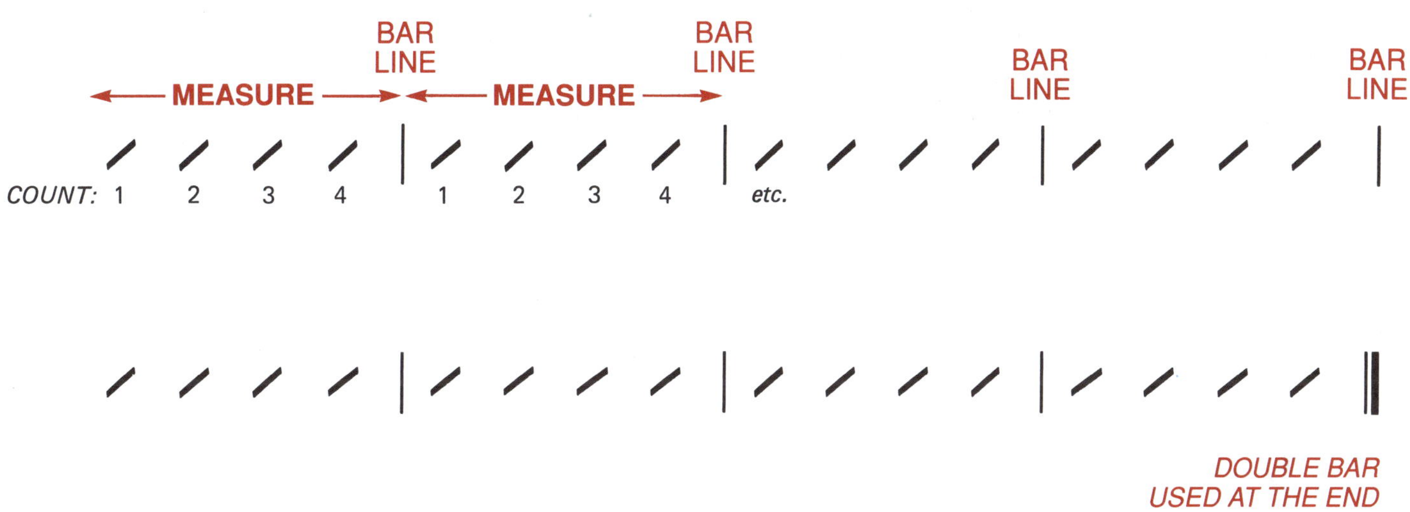

6. Push the STOP button to stop the Rhythm.

Getting Acquainted with the Keyboard

Auto: OFF Rhythm: OFF (Do not press START!) Register: PIANO

The black keys are in groups of 2's and 3's.

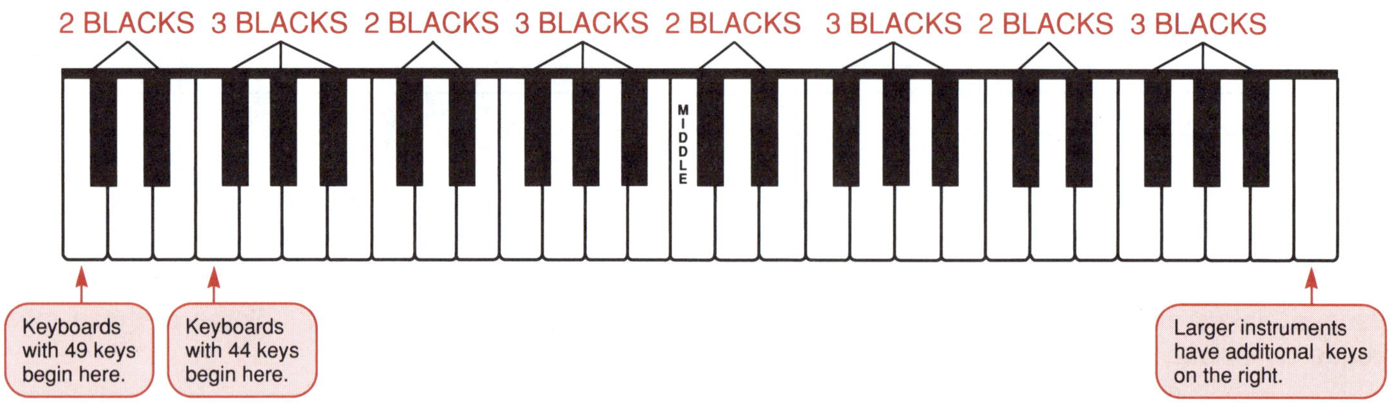

1. Play all the groups of THREE BLACK KEYS, with LH 4, 3 & 2. Begin with the keys on the left and move to the right. Play slowly, one key at a time, and listen! Notice that the tones sound higher and higher as you move from left to right.

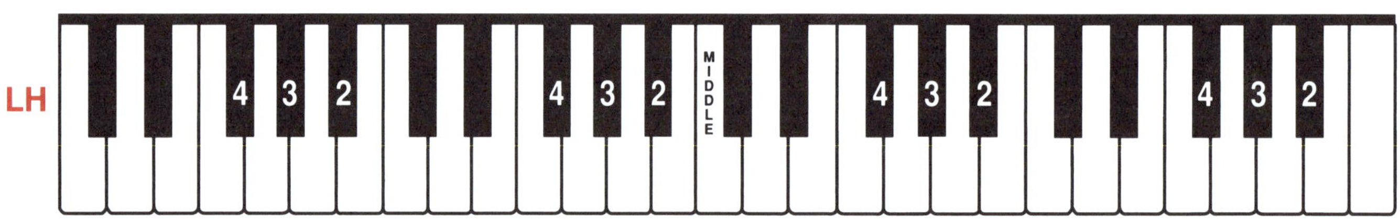

2. Play all the groups of TWO BLACK KEYS, using LH 3 & 2, one key at a time, moving from left to right.

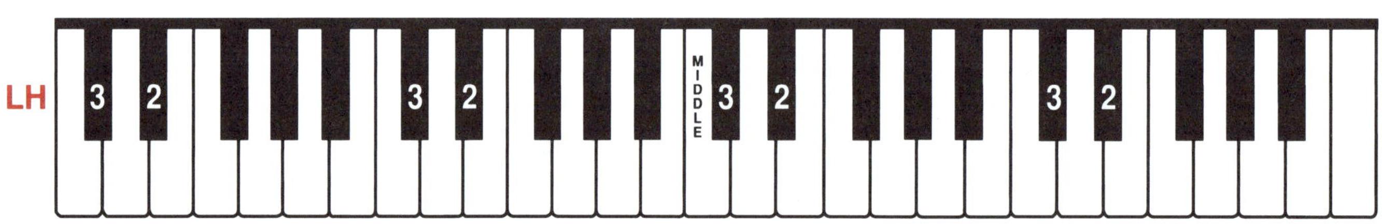

3. Play all the groups of THREE BLACK KEYS, with RH 2, 3 & 4, one key at a time, moving from left to right.

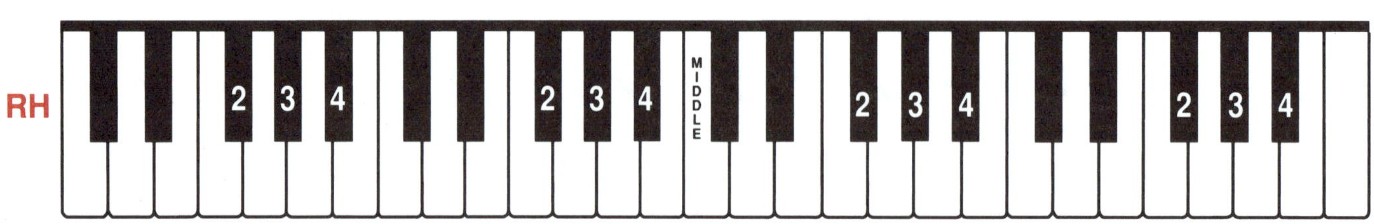

4. Play all the groups of TWO BLACK KEYS, using RH 2 & 3, one key at a time, moving from left to right.

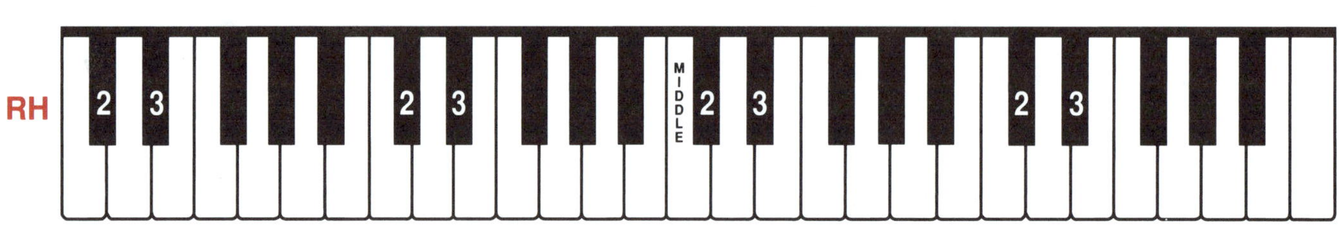

The Accompaniment (Auto) Section

The "Single Finger" chord setting on your instrument makes it very easy for your left hand to play a professional-sounding background for your right hand melodies. This will include basses and chords synchronized with any of the Rhythms you choose, and you can do it using only ONE FINGER of the left hand!

The ACCOMPANIMENT SECTION of your instrument is the portion of the keyboard on the LEFT that has the name of each white key indicated, as shown in the following diagram. (Some keyboards have the sharps and/or flats also indicated.)

To use this feature, turn on the Automatic Chords with the "Single Finger" setting. This will be indicated by **Auto:** ON "Single Finger" in this book.

IMPORTANT! Turn up the volume of the AUTO BASS CHORD section about half way.
You can adjust it later to your own taste.

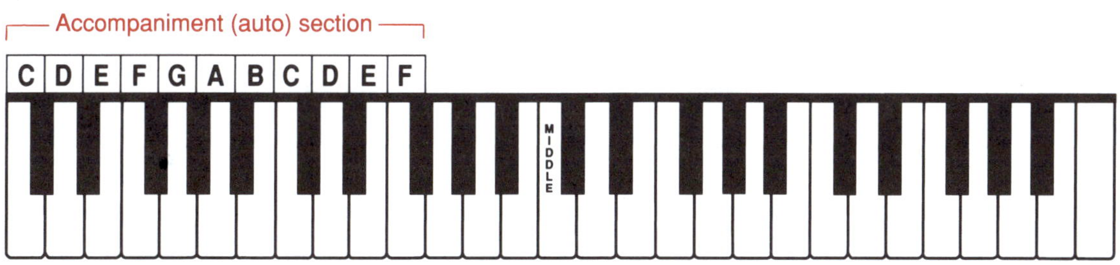

Fun with Auto Chord ON

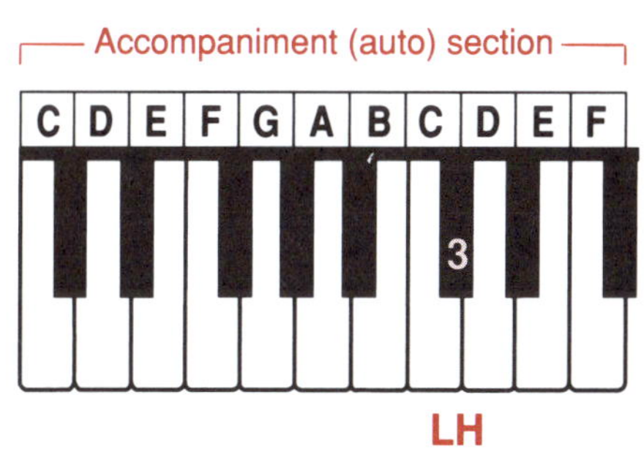

The exercise below will add a bass and chord accompaniment to any rhythm you choose. Count just as you did on page 7, ONE COUNT for each slash-mark.

In this exercise, you will play only the left black key of a two-black-key group, as shown in this keyboard diagram. Use LH 3.

Auto: ON "Single Finger" **Register:** Moderately slow SWING or slow MARCH.
Note: The Register setting has no effect on the accompaniment (Auto Chord) section!

Press SYNCHRO/START. Press the left key of the two-black-key group shown above, with LH 3. The moment you touch the key, the music will begin. YOU DO NOT NEED TO HOLD THE KEY DOWN. The accompaniment will continue until you press STOP!

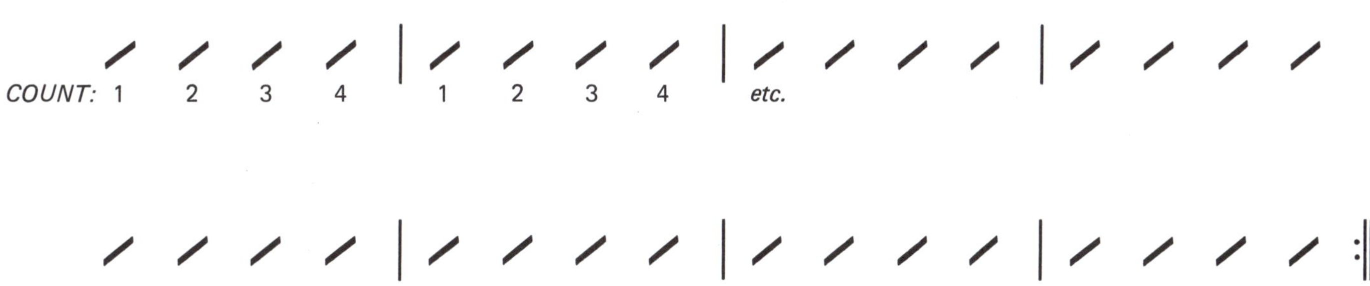

Quarter Notes & Half Notes

Music is made up of **short** tones and **long** tones. We write these tones in **notes,** and we measure their lengths by **counting.** The combining of notes into patterns is called RHYTHM.

Quarter Note
a **short** note.
COUNT: "1"
OR: "Quarter"

Half Note
a **long** note.
COUNT: "1 - 2"
OR: "Half-note"

Clap (or tap) the following rhythm. Clap ONCE for each note, counting aloud.
Notice how the BAR LINES divide the music into MEASURES of equal duration.

Two Black Keys

This piece uses the two-black-key group nearest the middle of your keyboard.
Play them with RH 2 & 3.

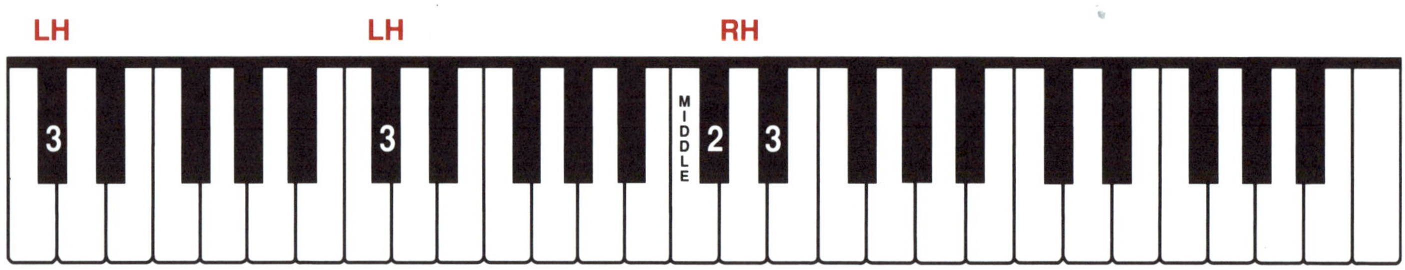

Auto: ON "Single Finger" **Rhythm:** OFF (Do not press START!) **Register:** PIANO

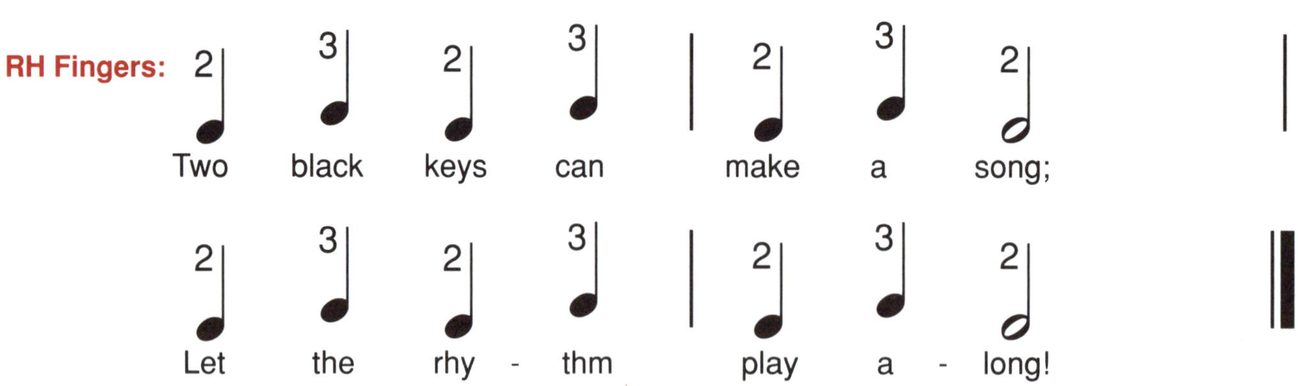

ADD RHYTHM
Select **Rhythm**: MARCH or SWING. Adjust to a rather SLOW tempo. Turn up RHYTHM VOLUME.
Press START, listen to a few measures, then play the RH shown above in time with the Rhythm.

ADD ACCOMPANIMENT
Select **Auto:** ON "Single Finger." Turn up AUTO BASS CHORD VOLUME.
Press SYNCHRO/START. Touch the left key of the lowest TWO-BLACK-KEY GROUP with LH 3. Listen to a few measures, then play the RH shown above again in time with the accompaniment. Remember, you do not have to hold down the LH.

Three Black Keys

This piece uses the three-black-key group just above (to the right of) the middle of your keyboard.
Play them with RH 2, 3, 4.

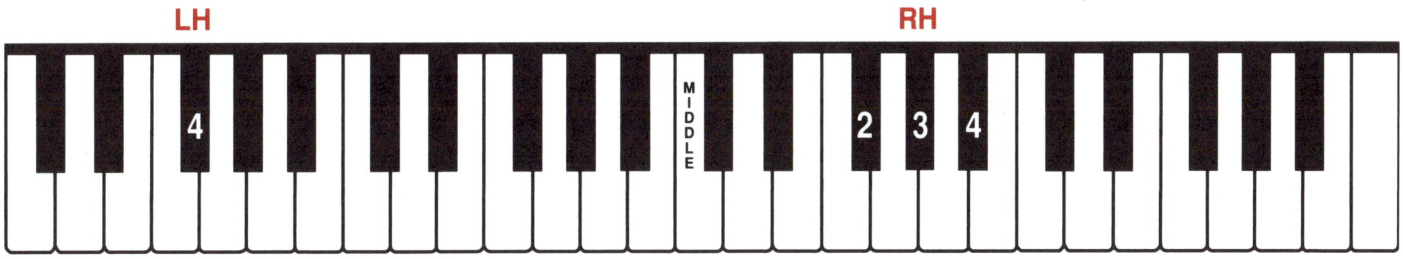

Auto: OFF **Rhythm:** OFF (Do not press START!) **Register:** PIANO

RH Fingers:

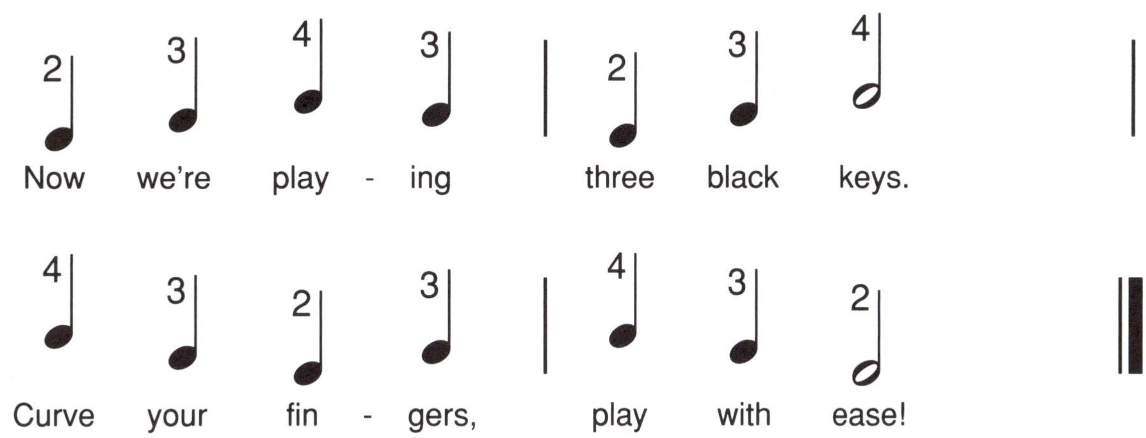

ADD RHYTHM

Repeat, using **Rhythm:** slow MARCH or SWING.
Press START. Listen to a few measures, adjust TEMPO, then play the RH again.

ADD ACCOMPANIMENT

Play again, with **Auto:** ON "Single Finger"
Press SYNCHRO/START. Touch the lowest BLACK KEY of the first THREE-BLACK-KEY GROUP (on the left) with LH 4. Listen to a few measures, then play the RH again.

Adding SPECIAL EFFECTS

Your instrument probably has one or more of the following special effects:

SUSTAIN VARIATION DUET ARPEGGIO

SUSTAIN causes the tones to linger after you have released the keys. This is especially effective on the following registers: PIANO, VIBES, HARPSICHORD, MUSIC BOX, GUITAR. On some instruments the difference in the sustained effect is more pronounced than on others. The SUSTAIN button has no effect on the Automatic accompaniment.

VARIATION adds different bass and rhythmic chord patterns to the Automatic accompaniment.

DUET adds a harmonizing note to each melody note when the Automatic accompaniment is being used.

ARPEGGIO adds broken chords running up and down. On some instruments these sound automatically unless you turn the ARPEGGIO volume all the way DOWN.

IMPORTANT!

Play *TWO BLACK KEYS* and *THREE BLACK KEYS* again, with slow MARCH or SWING Rhythm, and with **Auto:** ON "Single Finger," trying each of the special effects found on your instrument.
Repeat with various Registers.

Naming the Keys

Keys are named for the first seven letters of the alphabet, beginning with A.

A B C D E F G

Each white key is recognized by its position in or next to a black-key group!
For example: **A**'s are found between the **TOP TWO KEYS** of each **THREE-BLACK-KEY GROUP.**

Auto: OFF **Rhythm:** OFF **Register:** PIANO **Sustain:** ON

Play the following. Use LH 2 for keys below the middle of the keyboard.
Use RH 2 for keys above the middle of the keyboard.
Say the name of each key aloud as you play!

Play all the A's on your keyboard.

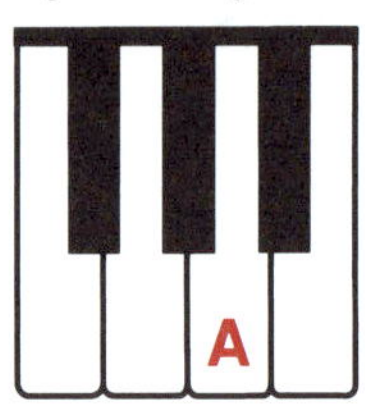

Play all the B's.

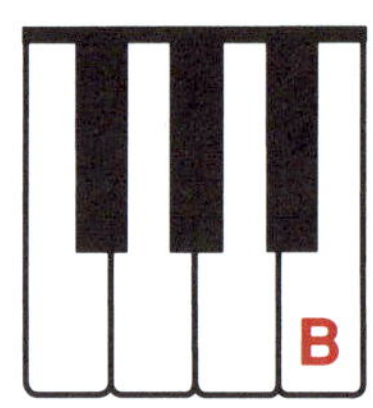

Play all the C's.

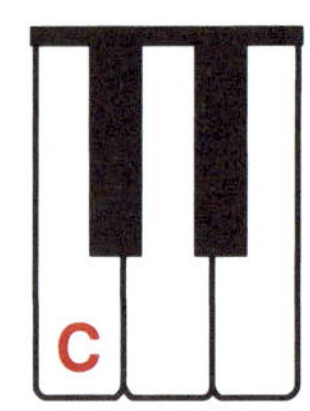

Play all the D's.

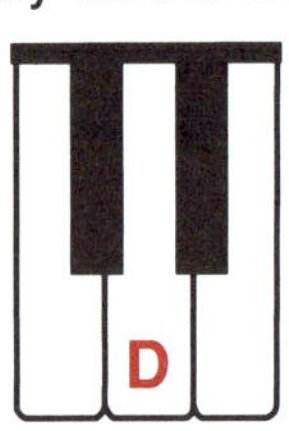

Play all the E's.

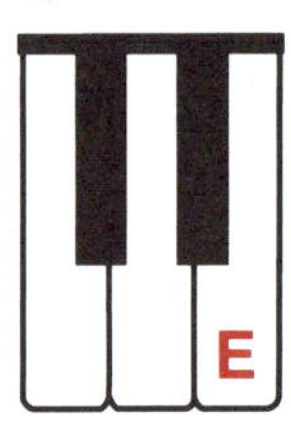

Play all the F's.

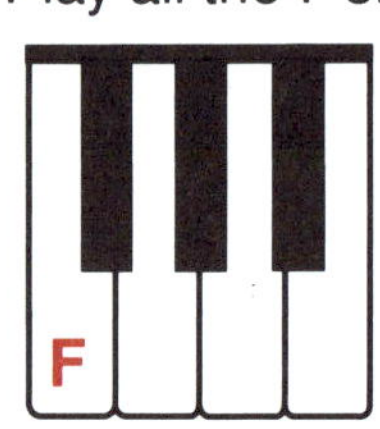

Play all the G's.

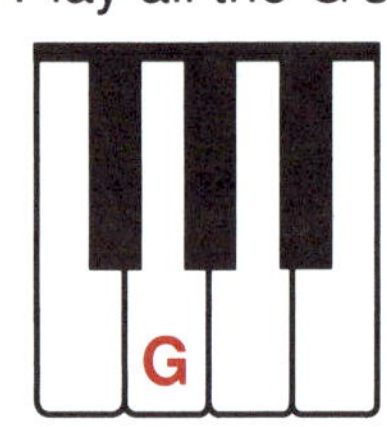

You can now name every white key on your instrument!

The key names are **A B C D E F G,** used over and over!

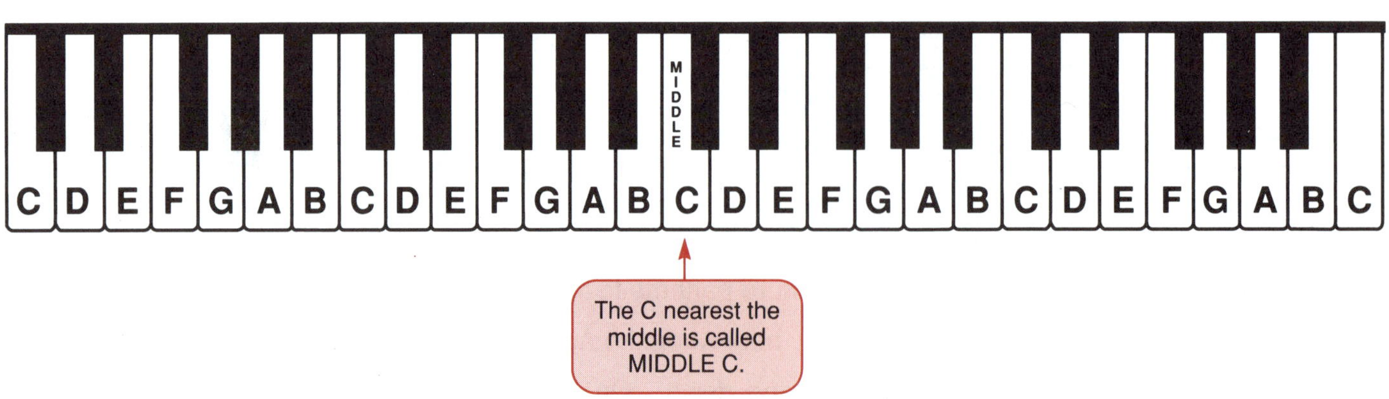

Going **UP** the keyboard, the notes sound **HIGHER and HIGHER!**

IMPORTANT! Play and name each white key, beginning with the lowest key (on the left).
Use LH 2 for keys below middle C, and RH 2 for keys above middle C.

Right Hand C Position

Place the RH on the keyboard so the **1st FINGER** falls on **MIDDLE C.**
Let the remaining 4 fingers fall naturally on the next 4 white keys.
Keep the fingers curved and relaxed.

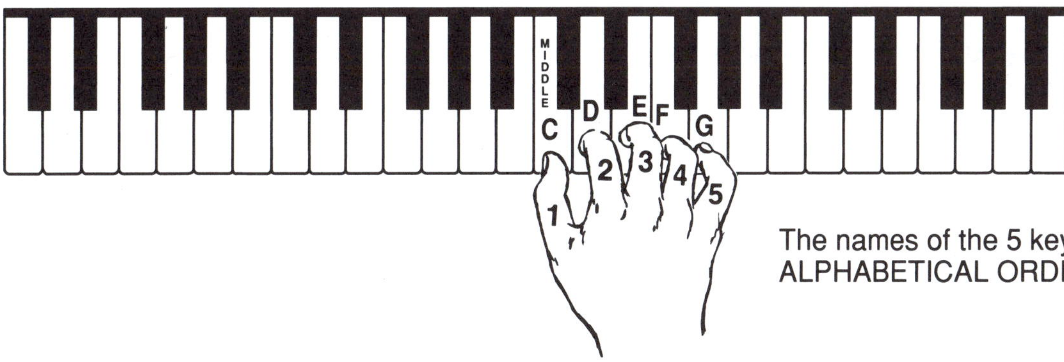

The names of the 5 keys are in ALPHABETICAL ORDER: **C D E F G.**

Notes for this position are written on the TREBLE STAFF

The TREBLE STAFF has 5 lines and 4 spaces.

Middle C is written on a short line below the staff, called a *leger* line D is written in the space below the staff. Each next higher note is written on the next higher line or space.

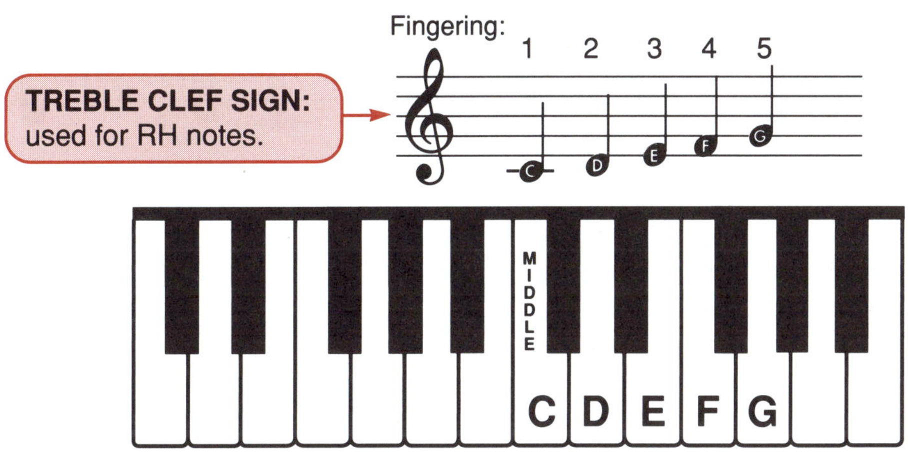

RIGHT HAND WARM-UP

Auto: OFF
Rhythm: OFF
Register: PIANO
Sustain: ON

Play the following *WARM-UP.* Say the name of each note aloud as you play.
Repeat until you can play smoothly and evenly. As the notes go higher on the keyboard, they are written higher on the staff! LOOK AT THE MUSIC, NOT THE KEYBOARD!

ODE TO JOY *(Theme from Beethoven's 9th Symphony)*

Auto: OFF **Rhythm:** OFF **Register:** ORGAN **Sustain:** OFF

1. Play with RH, counting aloud.
2. Play again and sing (or say) the note names.
3. Play again with a different Register of your own choice.

LOOK AT THE MUSIC, NOT THE KEYBOARD!

Fingers:

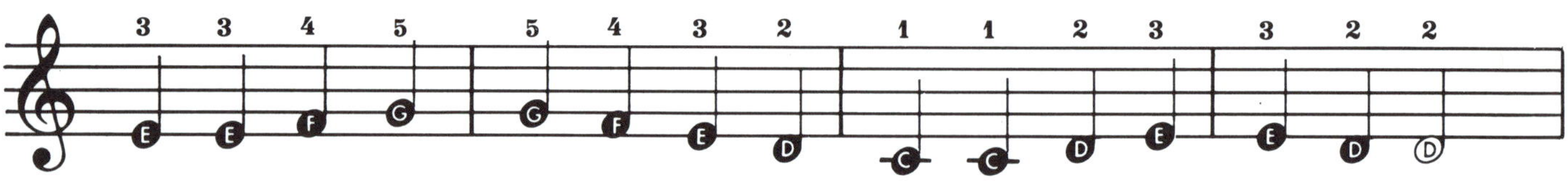

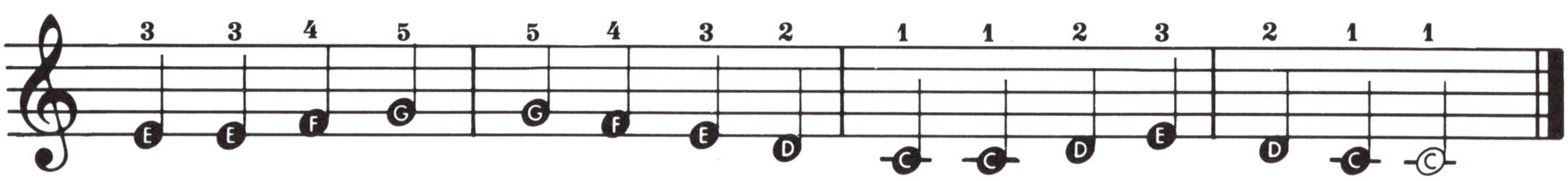

ADD RHYTHM

Play *ODE TO JOY* using **Rhythm:** slow MARCH.

Press START, listen to a few measures, adjust tempo, then play.

ADD SUSTAIN

Use **Register:** PIANO, with SUSTAIN. Try other Registers with SUSTAIN.

NOTE: In the original melody of *ODE TO JOY,* the last measure of each line is played with the first note held a little longer and the second note played a little shorter. This rhythm would be indicated:

longer shorter

Play it this way, if you wish.

MEMORY or RECORDING FEATURE

Some instruments have a "Real-time Melody Memory" that can be used to record a single-line melody you play on the keyboard. If your instrument has this feature, you may wish to use it to record your RH melodies and listen to them as they are played back. You can slow them down or speed them up with the tempo switch, if you wish.

Some more expensive instruments have sophisticated built-in sequencers (digital recording devices) that can record all the notes you play with both hands, including the auto rhythms and chords. Check your owner's manual for instructions on operating these features.

The Whole Note

Clap (or tap) the following rhythm.
Clap **ONCE** for each note, counting aloud.

Whole Note

a **very long** note.

COUNT: "1 - 2 - 3 - 4"

Row, Row, Row Your Boat

(RIGHT SIDE UP AND UPSIDE DOWN)

The first line is the familiar tune.
The second line is the same, upside down!

Auto: OFF **Rhythm:** OFF **Register:** PIANO, ORGAN or GUITAR **Sustain:** OFF

1. Clap (or tap) the rhythm, counting aloud. Count evenly.
2. Play with RH, singing (or saying) the finger numbers.
3. Play and count.
4. Play and sing (or say) the note names.

ADD RHYTHM

Use **Rhythm:** Slow MARCH or SWING.
Press START. Listen to a few measures, adjust TEMPO, then play *ROW, ROW, ROW* with RH, along with the Rhythm. Press STOP at the end.

ADD ACCOMPANIMENT

The accompaniment keys, on the left, have the names of the white keys printed above the back edge of the keyboard. Since you have already learned to identify each of the white keys, these key names are not necessary, but they may be helpful in the beginning.

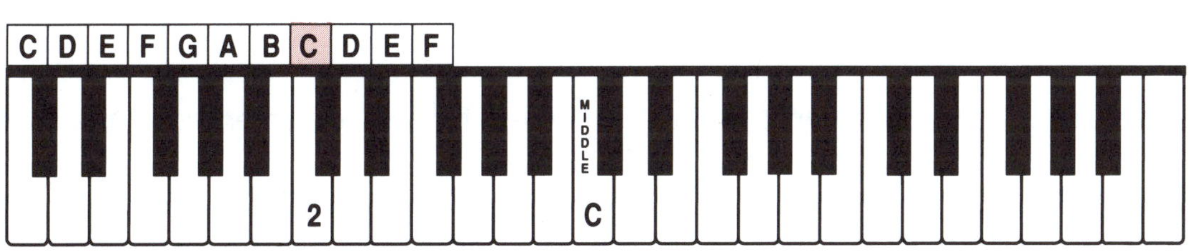

Use **Auto:** ON "Single Finger." Press SYNCHRO/START. Touch the C below middle C with LH 2 (you need not hold the key down). Listen to a few measures, then play *ROW, ROW, ROW YOUR BOAT* with RH, along with the accompaniment. When you finish, press the ENDING button, if available. If not, press STOP.

The Time Signature

Music has numbers at the beginning called the **TIME SIGNATURE.**

The **TOP NUMBER** tells the number of beats (counts) in each measure.
The **BOTTOM NUMBER** tells the kind of note that gets ONE beat (count).

4 = **4** beats to each measure.
4 = **QUARTER NOTE** ♩ gets ONE beat.

		COUNT	TOTAL NUMBER OF COUNTS
QUARTER NOTE	♩	"1"	1
HALF NOTE	𝅗𝅥	"1 - 2"	2
WHOLE NOTE	𝅝	"1 - 2 - 3 - 4"	4

Note-Reading Made Easy!

1. Find the starting note. If the next note is on the same line or space, play the same key again. If the note moves UP on the staff, play a higher key. If the note moves DOWN on the staff, play a LOWER key.

Auto: OFF **Rhythm:** OFF **Register:** PIANO, ORGAN, or GUITAR **Sustain:** OFF

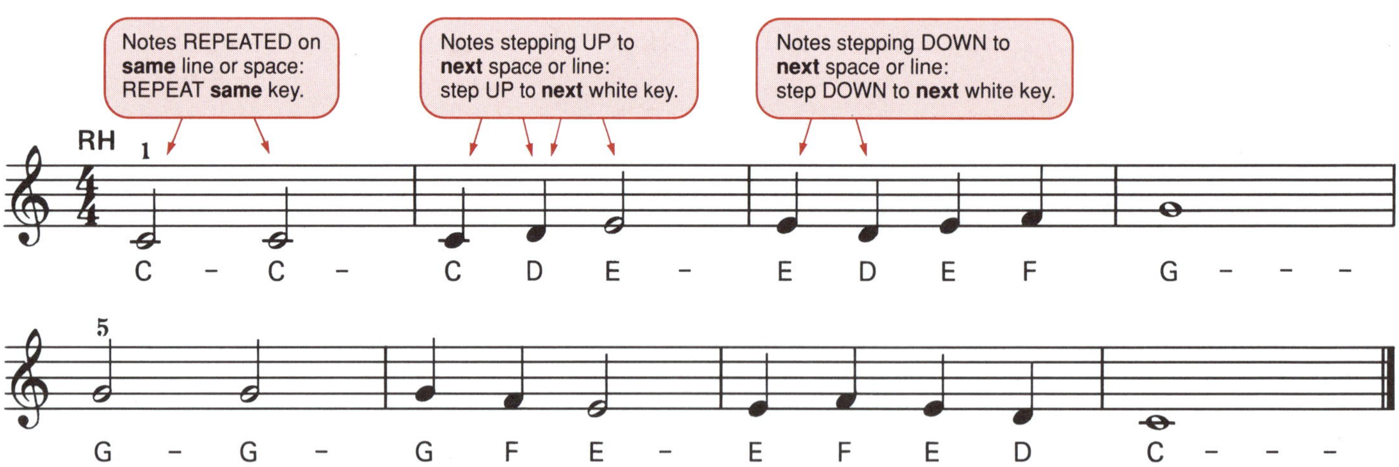

2. Repeat several times, using a different Register each time. Try each Register with **Sustain:** OFF and with **Sustain:** ON.
3. Add **Rhythm:** Slow MARCH, SWING, POP, or COUNTRY. Press START, then play.
4. Add Accompaniment. Use **Auto:** ON "Single Finger." Press SYNCHRO/START. Touch the C below middle C with LH 2 ***exactly*** when you begin to play the RH melody. Press the ENDING button or STOP at the end.
5. Add VARIATION and/or DUET, and play again.

Repeated Notes

Notes repeated on the same line or space repeat the same key on the keyboard.

Auto: OFF **Rhythm:** OFF **Register:** PIANO **Sustain:** OFF

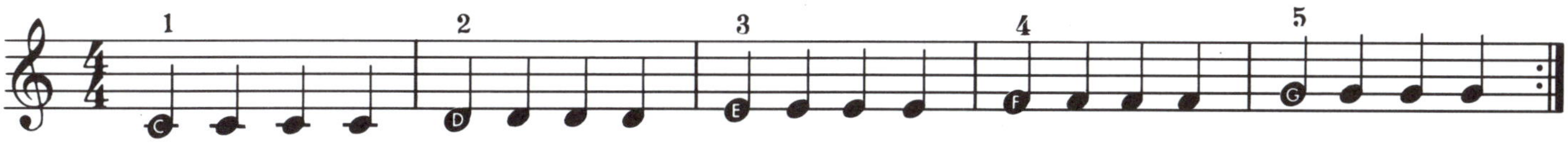

The DOUBLE DOTS mean REPEAT FROM THE BEGINNING.

Intervals: 2nds

Distances from one note to another are measured in INTERVALS, called 2nds, 3rds, etc.

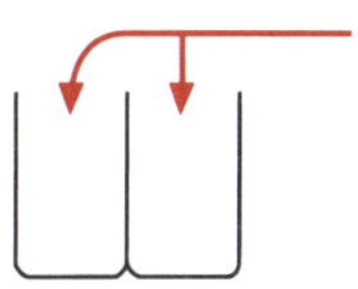

The distance from any white key to the next white key, up or down, is called a **2nd.**

2nds are written LINE-SPACE or SPACE-LINE.

Play, saying "UP a 2nd," etc.

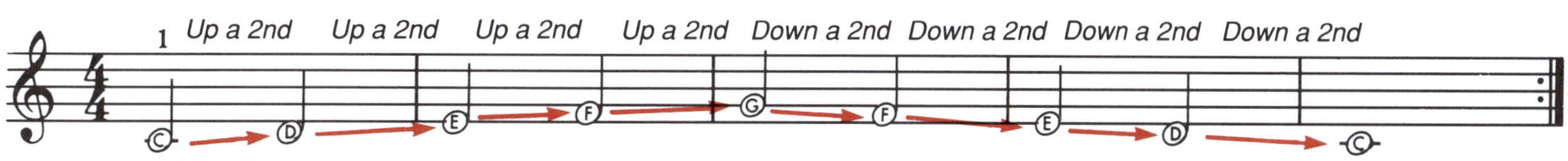

SLUR: or

SLURS mean play LEGATO.
LEGATO means SMOOTHLY CONNECTED.

SECONDS

Auto: OFF **Rhythm:** OFF **Register:** PIANO **Sustain:** ON

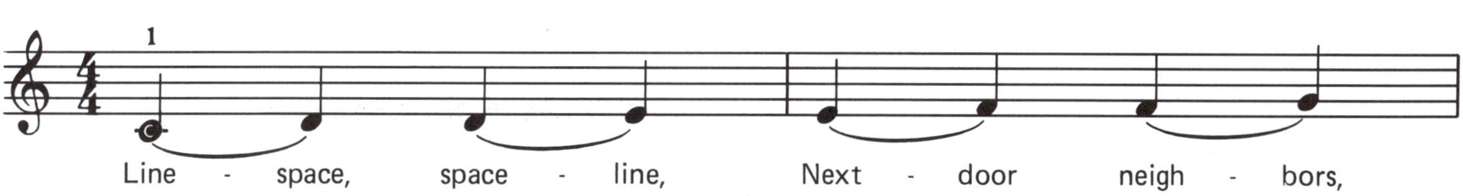

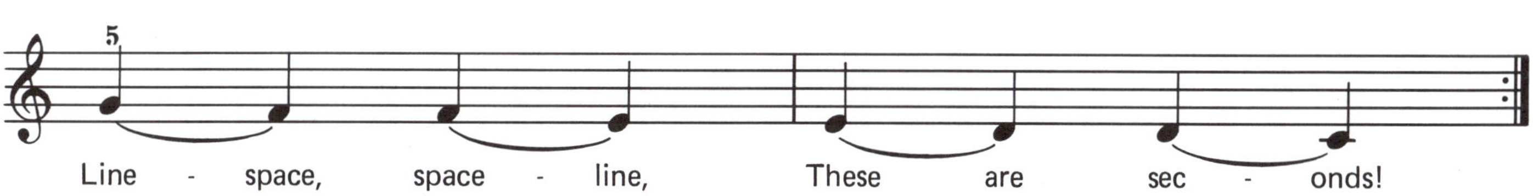

ADD RHYTHM

Use **Rhythm:** Slow MARCH or SWING. (Be sure the Rhythm VOLUME is turned up!) Press START. Listen to a few measures, adjust TEMPO, then add RH. Play several times, then press STOP.

Reading Notes by Intervals

To play the following music it is not necessary to read each note by name. If you know the starting note and finger number, you will find it easy to play the entire piece by simply observing the following:

- Does the note REPEAT on the same line or space? If is does, REPEAT the SAME KEY.
- Does the note go UP to the next line or space? If it does, play the next key to the RIGHT.
- Does the note move DOWN to the next line or space? If it does, play the next key to the LEFT.

Notes always make the same patterns on the keyboard as they do on the music. When you play this way, you will be reading music like a professional!

THE SECOND STREET BAND **(Melody Only)**

Auto: OFF **Rhythm** OFF **Register:** GUITAR, PIANO or VIBES **Sustain:** OFF

1. Play several times with RH. Begin with 1 on middle C, and read by INTERVALS!

2. Repeat several times, using a different Register each time.

Changing Chords in the Accompaniment

When you play any key in the accompaniment section with **Auto:** ON "Single Finger," the accompaniment will continue to sound after you release the key. This gives you time to move easily from one chord to the next.

The following LH position will allow you to move easily from C to G.
Be sure LH 2 is over C. LH 5 will then fall naturally on G.

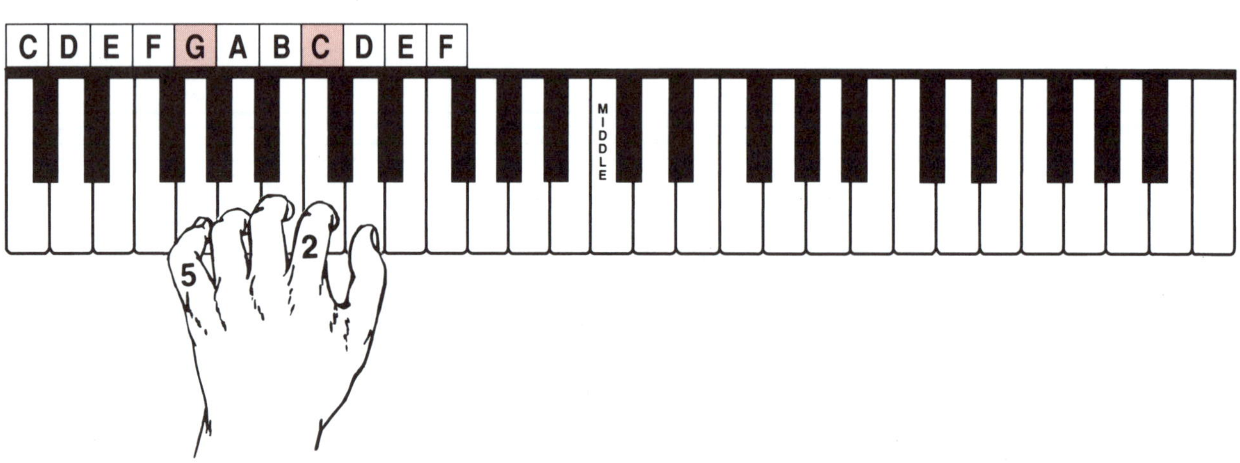

The key to be touched with the LH to produce any MAJOR CHORD accompaniment is indicated by a CAPITAL LETTER above the treble staff. In this book these letters are printed in RED. Be careful to touch ONLY the indicated key! If you even slightly touch a neighboring key, an incorrect chord will sound.

Left Hand Warm-Up

Auto: ON "Single Finger" **Rhythm:** Slow MARCH, SWING or COUNTRY

1. Press SYNCHRO/START.
2. Counting FOUR for each measure (ONE count for each slash-mark), touch the LH key indicated in red on the first count of each measure over which it appears. Remember, you do not have to hold the key down. This gives you plenty of time to think about playing the next key.

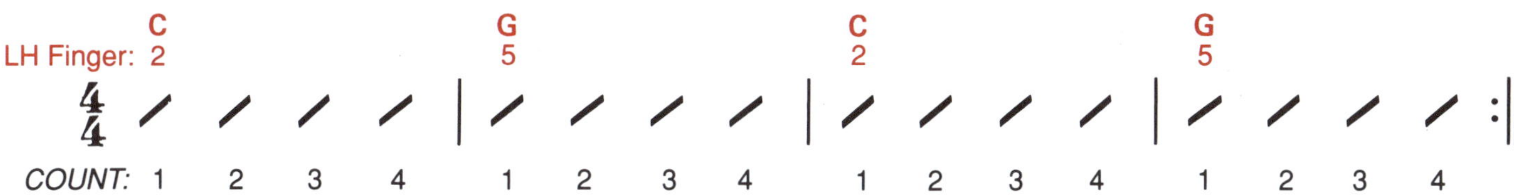

The Second Street Band
(Melody and "Single Finger Chord" Accompaniment)

Auto: ON "Single Finger" **Rhythm:** Slow MARCH, SWING or COUNTRY
Register: PIANO, VIBES or GUITAR **Sustain:** OFF

1. Play the LH accompaniment alone. Count FOUR for each measure, playing the indicated key on the first count of the measure over which the red letter C or G appears. Press SYNCHRO/START and begin.
2. Play with hands together. Press SYNCHRO/START and begin.

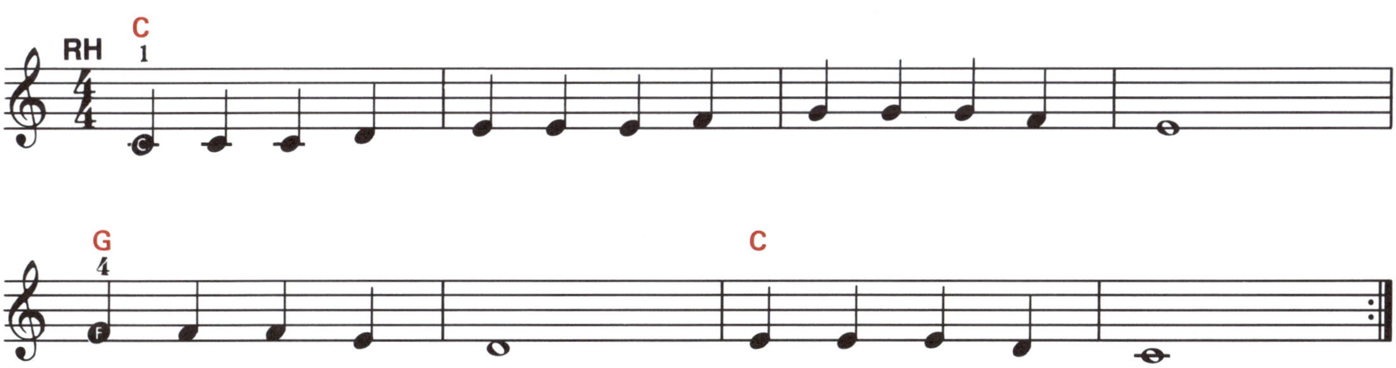

3. Play again, adding VARIATION, DUET or other effects. Use any register you choose. Use **Sustain:** OFF or ON, as you wish.

Four Ways to END a Song

1. For a quick stop at the end, press the STOP button just after the last count.
2. To hold the last chord at the end, play the key for the last chord on the last measure of the piece. Press the STOP button with RH on the third count of the last measure, while still holding the LH key.
3. FADE. Let the accompaniment continue after the piece is over, and gradually turn down the MASTER VOLUME.
4. Some instruments have an ENDING button. Press it on the first count of the last measure.

Intervals: 3rds

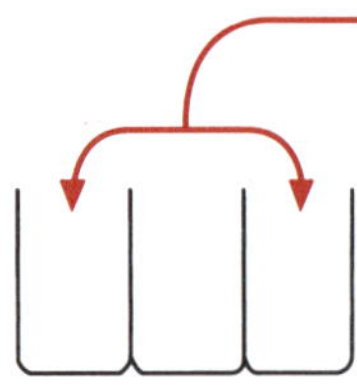

When you skip a white key, the interval is a **3rd.**

3rds are written LINE-LINE or SPACE-SPACE.

Play, saying "UP a 3rd," etc.

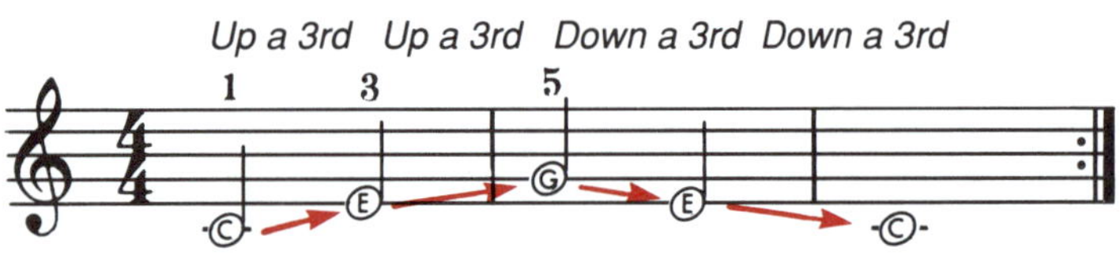

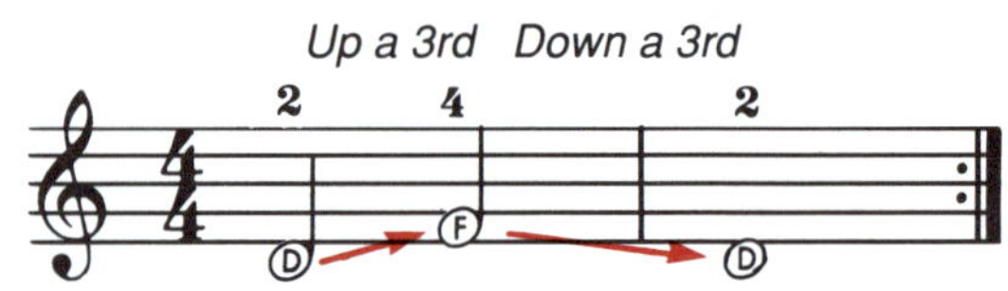

THIRDS

Auto: ON "Single Finger"
Rhythm: Moderately Slow MARCH, SWING or COUNTRY

Register: PIANO, MUSIC BOX or GUITAR
Sustain: ON

1. Play RH alone, without Auto Rhythm (do not press START).
2. Add Rhythm: Press START, adjust TEMPO. Count "1-2-3-4" for a few measures, then play.

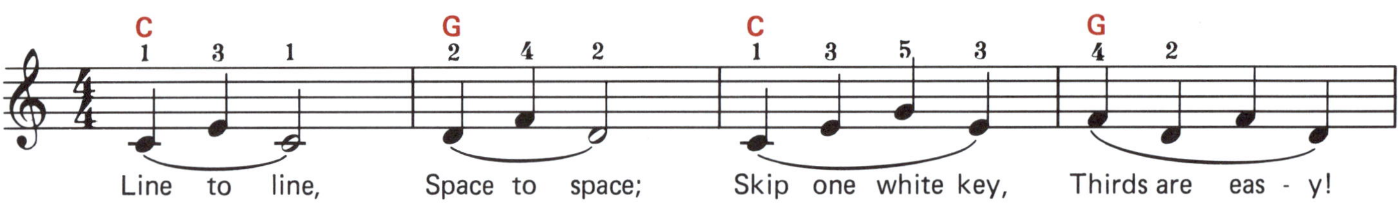

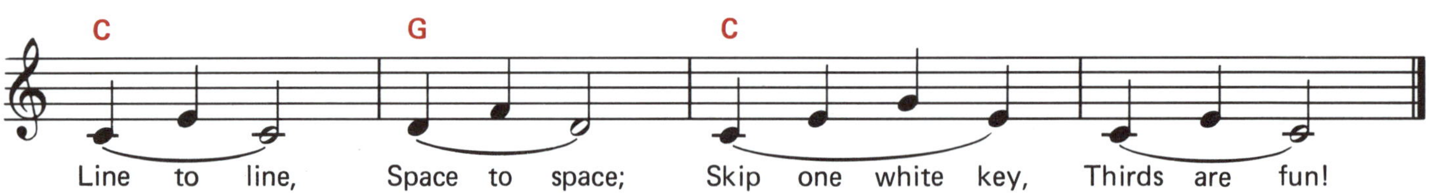

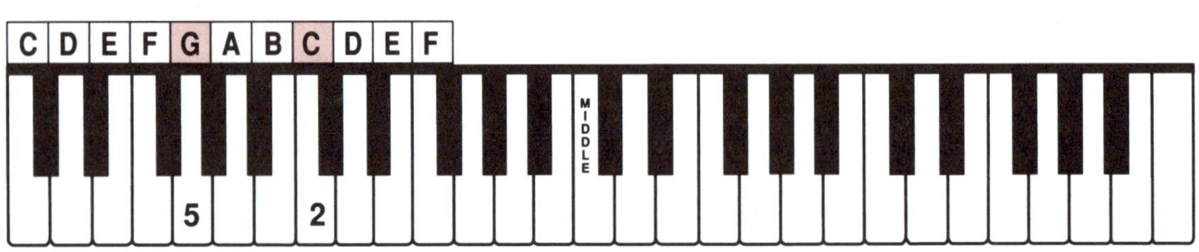

3. Add LH accompaniment: Press SYNCHRO (SYNCHRO/START), then begin. Press STOP, or use ENDING button at the end.
4. Play again, adding VARIATION, DUET and any other effect you wish.
5. Play again, using a different Register.
6. (OPTIONAL) Play again, using a different Rhythm (any Rhythm except WALTZ).

DYNAMIC SIGNS: ***p***, ***mf***, ***f***, tell how SOFT or LOUD to play.
Some instruments are "touch sensitive," like a piano. When you play with more weight, the key descends faster and the tone is louder. On instruments not so equipped, you must adjust the MASTER VOLUME CONTROL before you begin to play.

p (piano) = SOFT

Au Claire de la Lune

Auto: OFF
Rhythm: Slow SWING or MARCH
Register: FLUTE, PICCOLO or CLARINET
Sustain: OFF

1. Adjust volume to SOFT.
2. Play without Auto Rhythm. (Do not press START.)
3. Add Rhythm. Press START. Listen. Adjust TEMPO. Count "1-2-3-4," then begin.
4. Play again, using PIANO or MUSIC BOX, with Sustain ON.

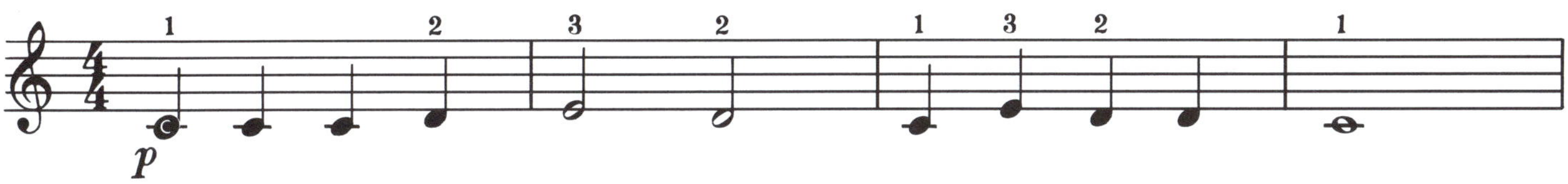

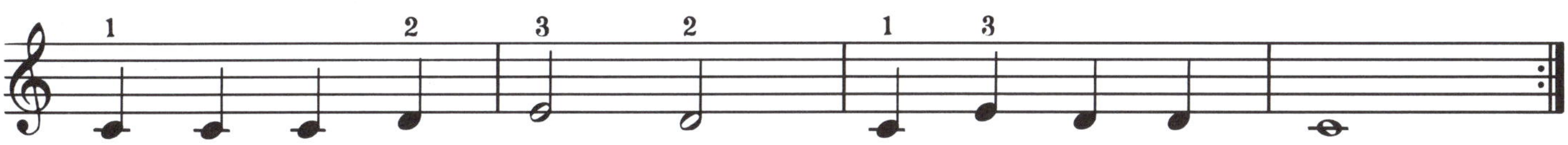

mf (mezzo forte) = *MODERATELY LOUD*

Join the Fun!

Auto: ON "Single Finger"
Rhythm: Moderately slow SWING or MARCH
Register: PIANO
Sustain: ON

1. Adjust volume to MODERATELY LOUD.
2. Play RH alone, without Auto Rhythm. (Do not press START.)
3. Add Rhythm. Press START. Listen. Adjust TEMPO. Count "1-2-3-4," then play.
4. Add LH accompaniment. Press SYNCHRO, then begin.

5. Add VARIATION, DUET and other effects.
6. Play with any other Rhythm except WALTZ.

Merrily We Roll Along

f (forte) = *LOUD*

Auto: ON "Single Finger"
Rhythm: Moderately slow SWING or MARCH

Register: PIANO
Sustain: ON

1. Adjust volume to LOUD.
2. Play RH alone, without Auto Rhythm. (Do not press START.)
3. Add Rhythm. Press START. Listen. Adjust TEMPO. Count "1-2-3-4," then begin.
4. Add LH accompaniment. Press SYNCHRO, then begin.

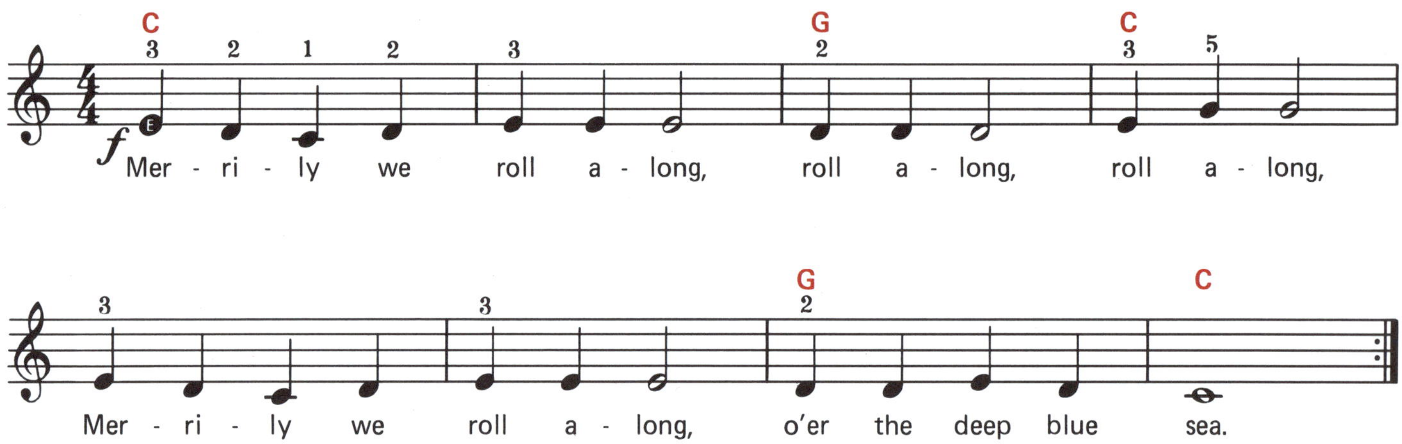

5. Add VARIATION, DUET and other effects.
6. Play with any other Rhythm except WALTZ.

DUET PART

For performance by the teacher or another student on the SAME KEYBOARD or a different one. This part may be programmed into the memory on instruments that have built-in sequencers. The student can then play along as the duet part is played back.

Hot Dog!

Auto: ON "Single Finger"
Rhythm: Moderately slow SWING or MARCH
Register: PIANO, VIBES or GUITAR
Sustain: ON

1. Play RH only.
2. Add Rhythm.
3. Add LH accompaniment. Use VARIATION, DUET and other effects, if you wish.

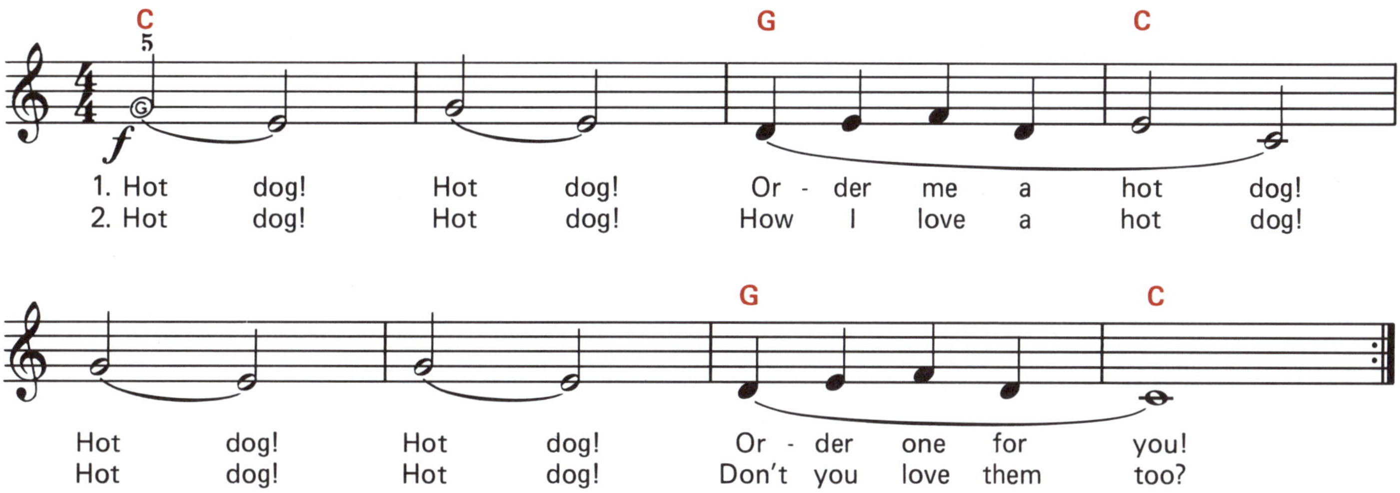

Playing with Sustained Accompaniment LH Chords

When **Auto:** ON "Single Finger" is used ***without*** pressing START or SYNCHRO/START, the LH chord is sustained as long as you hold the key down. No Rhythm background will be heard when you do this. Certain types of pieces, such as hymns and slow melodies, are often more effective when played with sustained LH chords.

When you play *LARGO,* hold the LH C until the G appears, then hold the G until the C appears, etc.

Largo *(from "The New World")*

This melody is also known as *GOING HOME.* The word *"LARGO"* means "very slow."

Auto: ON "Single Finger"
Rhythm: OFF
Register: ORGAN, TRUMPET or BRASS
Sustain: OFF

1. Play the LH sustained chords separately. (Do not press START or SYNCHRO/START.) Count "1-2-3-4" for each measure. The LH chords must not overlap or an incorrect chord will sound.
2. Play the RH alone.
3. Play hands together.

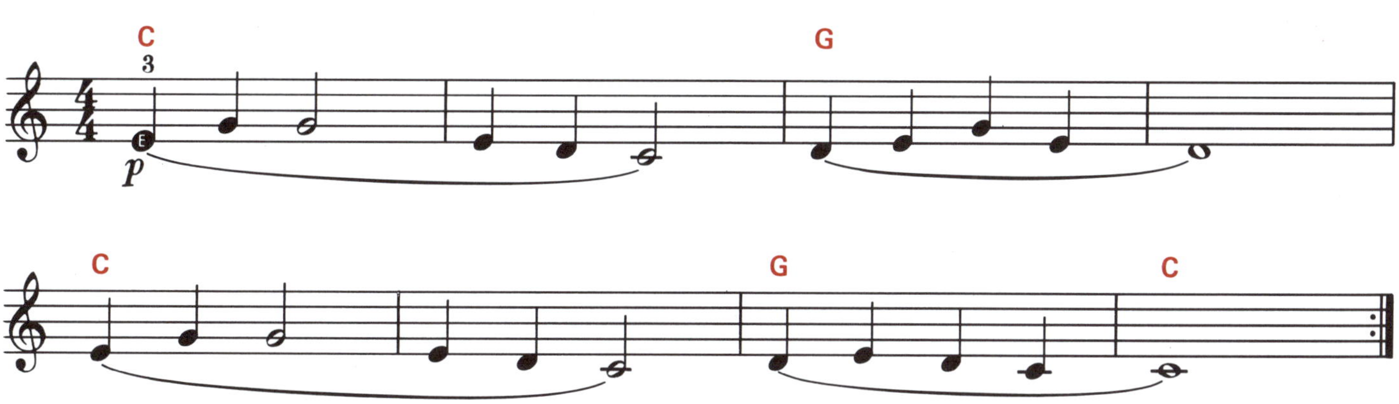

4. Add DUET, if available. (VARIATION does not function when Rhythm is OFF.)

Intervals: 4ths

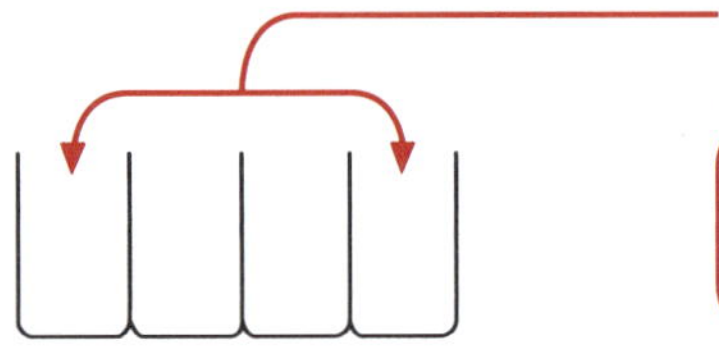

When you skip 2 white keys, the interval is a **4th.**

4ths are written LINE-SPACE, skipping a space, or SPACE-LINE, skipping a line.

Play, saying "UP a 4th," etc.

The F Chord

The LH accompaniment of the next few pieces will begin on the F MAJOR "Single Finger" chord.
Play the F below middle C with the 1st finger (thumb). C will be played with LH 2 and G with LH 5, as before.*

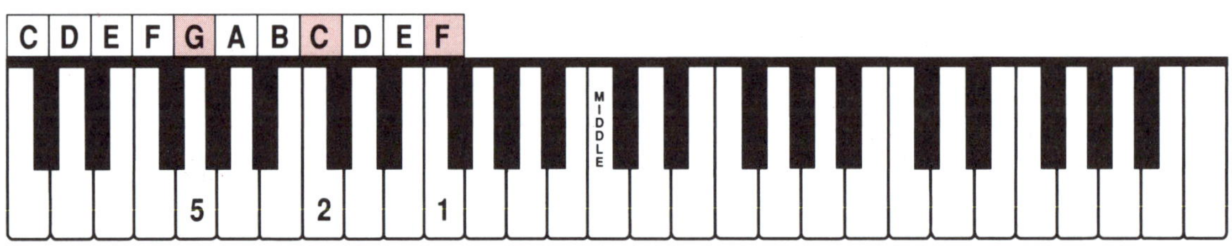

Play a Fourth!

Auto: ON "Single Finger"
Rhythm: OFF
Register: PIANO
Sustain: ON

1. Play RH alone.
2. Add LH, using SUSTAINED ACCOMPANIMENT. Hold each LH chord until the next letter appears.

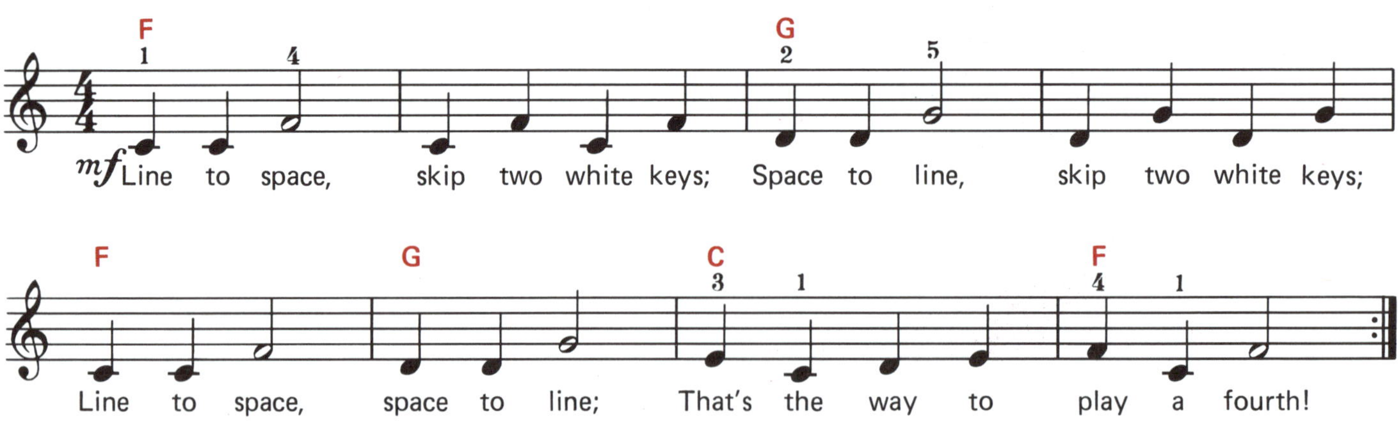

3. Add **Rhythm:** Moderately slow MARCH.
4. Add LH accompaniment. Press SYNCHRO, then begin.

*While this fingering sets up the best hand position for playing "Fingered Chords" (page 29), it is not absolutely necessary to play the "Single Finger Chords" this way. Any finger(s) the student is comfortable with is fine.

Fourths & Thirds

Auto: ON "Single Finger"
Rhythm: Moderately slow MARCH, SWING or POP

Register: PIANO
Sustain: ON

1. Play RH alone.
2. Add LH accompaniment. Press SYNCHRO and begin.
3. Add DUET and VARIATION, if you wish.

Aura Lee

This melody was made into a popular song, "*LOVE ME TENDER,*" sung by Elvis Presley.

1. Play RH alone.
2. Add LH, using SUSTAINED ACCOMPANIMENT. Hold each LH chord until the next letter appears.
3. Add DUET, if available.

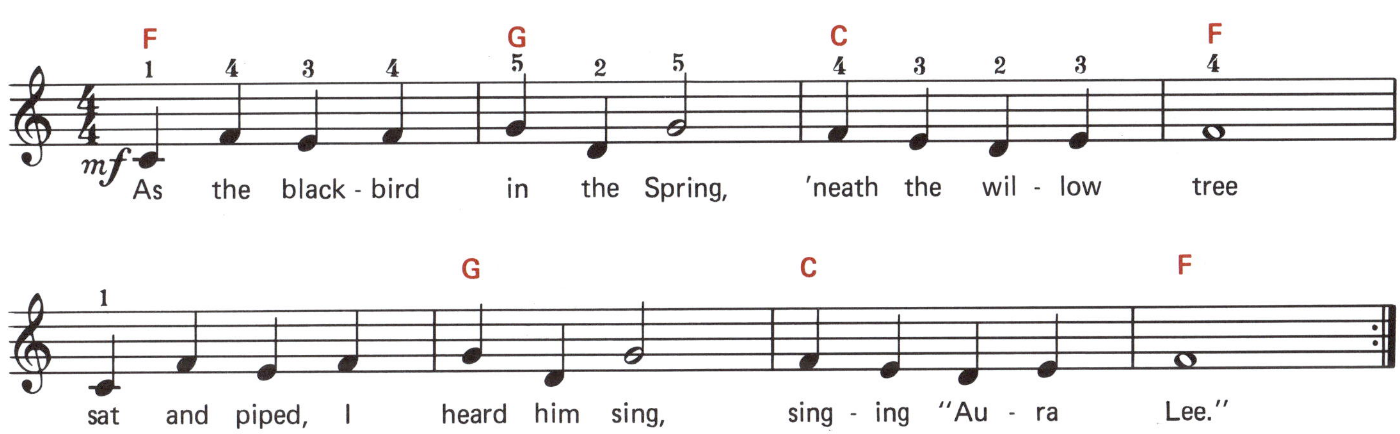

4. Add **Rhythm:** Moderately slow SWING or POP. Press SYNCHRO and play LH.
   (Reminder: You need not hold each LH key when playing with Auto Rhythm.
5. Add VARIATION or ARPEGGIO.

Intervals: 5ths

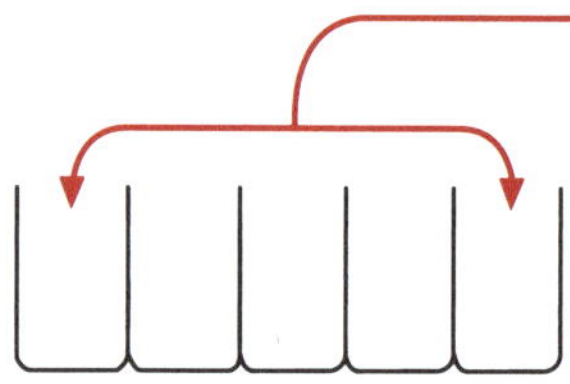

When you skip 3 white keys, the interval is a **5th.**

5ths are written LINE-LINE, skipping a line, or SPACE-SPACE, skipping a space.

Play, saying "UP a 5th, etc.

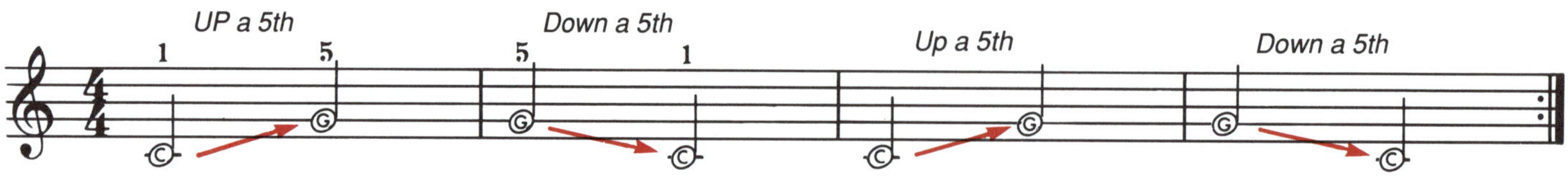

FIFTHS

Auto: ON "Single Finger"
Rhythm: Moderately slow SWING, ROCK or POP

Register: ORGAN with Sustain OFF, or PIANO with Sustain ON

1. Play RH alone.
2. Play with LH accompaniment. Press SYNCHRO and begin. You need only touch LH C. The chord is the same throughout the piece.

THE ONE-MAN BAND

Auto: ON "Single Finger"
Rhythm: Moderately fast SWING, ROCK or SLOW ROCK

Register: ORGAN
Sustain: OFF

1. Play RH alone, slowly. Count aloud.
2. Add Rhythm: Press START. Listen. Adjust TEMPO. Count "1-2-3-4," then begin.
3. Add LH: Press SYNCHRO, then begin.

This piece has only one LH chord.

4. Try other Rhythms. Use any Rhythm except WALTZ.
5. Add VARIATION and/or DUET.

How to Play "Single Finger" 7th Chords

The "Single Finger" 7th chord actually requires two or more fingers to play, depending on the make of instrument you use.

On CASIO and REALISTIC instruments, the 7th chord is made by playing THREE KEYS:

Play the KEY NOTE plus any TWO KEYS to the RIGHT, black or white. It is easiest to simply add the next TWO WHITE KEYS to the RIGHT.

For G⁷, play G, A & B. Use LH 5, 4 & 3. (No change in hand position is needed.)

G7

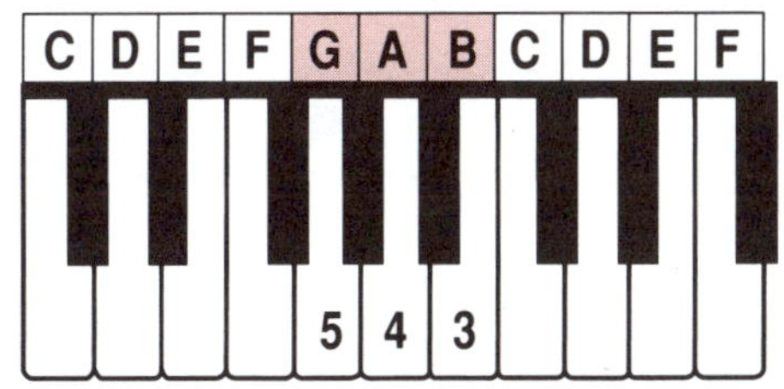

On YAMAHA, BALDWIN, and TECHNICS instruments, the 7th chord is made by playing TWO KEYS:

Play the KEY NOTE plus any WHITE KEY to the LEFT. It is easiest to simply add the next WHITE KEY to the LEFT.

For G⁷, play G and the next F to its left. Use LH 5 & 4. (Shift LH position ONE KEY TO THE LEFT!)

G7

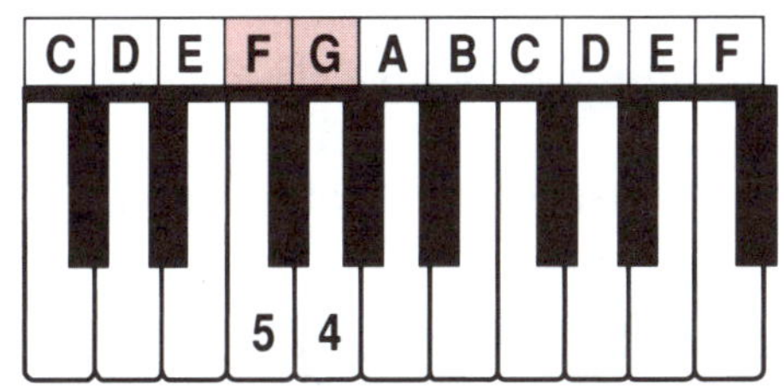

On LOWRY & new KAWAI keyboards, the G⁷ chord is made this way.

G⁷ Warm-Up

1. In order to hear the full sound of the chords, play this warm-up first with SUSTAINED ACCOMPANIMENT. Do not press START or SYNCHRO/START. You will not hear the chord repeated, but each chord will be sustained for four counts. Use **Auto:** ON "Single Finger."

   REMEMBER: Register changes do not effect the accompaniment section. Do not let LH chords overlap. Lift fingers from one chord before playing the next.

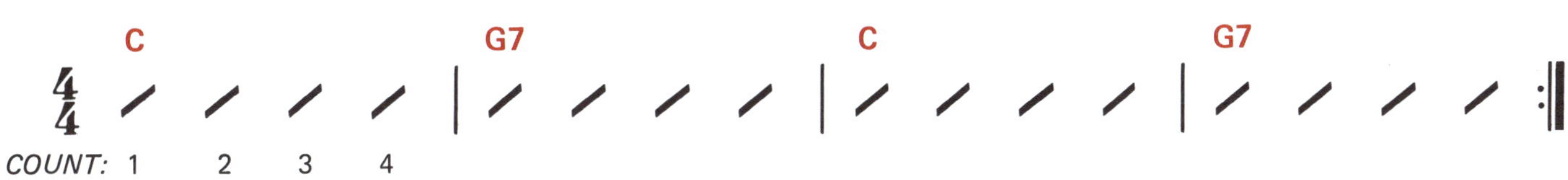

2. Add **Rhythm:** Slow SWING. Press SYNCHRO, then begin.

Here's a Happy Song!

Auto: ON "Single Finger"
Rhythm: Moderately fast SWING

Register: PIANO, MUSIC BOX or GUITAR
Sustain: ON

1. Play RH alone without Rhythm.
2. Add Rhythm: Press START. Adjust TEMPO. Count "1-2-3-4" for a few measures, then play RH again.
3. Add LH: Press SYNCHRO, then begin.

Happily

4. Add special effects, such as DUET and VARIATION, if you have them.
5. Play with COUNTRY, POP, or ROCK 'N' ROLL Rhythm.

TIED NOTES: When notes on the *same* line or space are joined with a curved line, we call them **TIED NOTES.**
The key is held down for the
COMBINED VALUES OF BOTH NOTES!

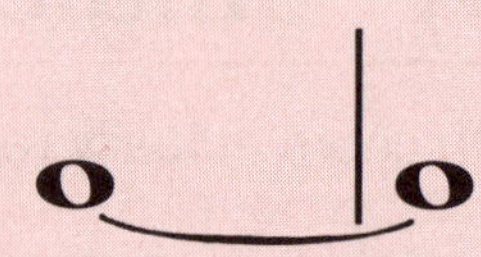

COUNT: "1 - 2 - 3 - 4,   1 - 2 - 3 - 4."

JOIN THE BAND!

Auto: ON "Single Finger"
Rhythm: Moderately slow MARCH

Register: ORGAN, SAX, TRUMPET or SYNTHE
Sustain: OFF

1. Play RH alone. Count aloud.
2. Add Rhythm.
3. Add LH: Press SYNCHRO, then begin. Be sure to play the LH F with 1 (the thumb).
4. Add special effects, such as DUET and VARIATION, if you have them.

5. Play with other Rhythms and Registers, adding any effects you choose.

Introducing B for Right Hand

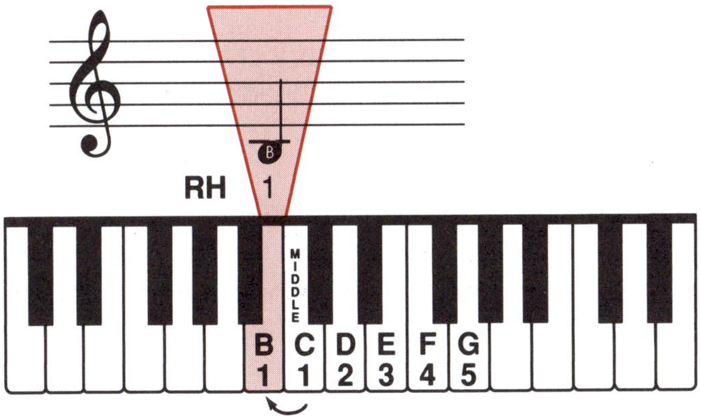

TO FIND B:
Place the RH in **C POSITION.**
Reach finger 1 one white key to the left!

Auto: OFF **Register:** PIANO
Rhythm: OFF **Sustain:** ON

Play slowly. Say the note names as you play.

MARY ANN

Auto: ON "Single Finger"
Rhythm: Moderately fast SWING, COUNTRY or ROCK 'N' ROLL
Register: TRUMPET with Sustain OFF or PIANO with Sustain ON

1. Play the RH alone several times, without Rhythm. Count aloud.
2. Add Rhythm: Press START. Adjust TEMPO. Count "1-2-3-4," then play RH again.
3. Add LH: Press SYNCHRO, then begin.

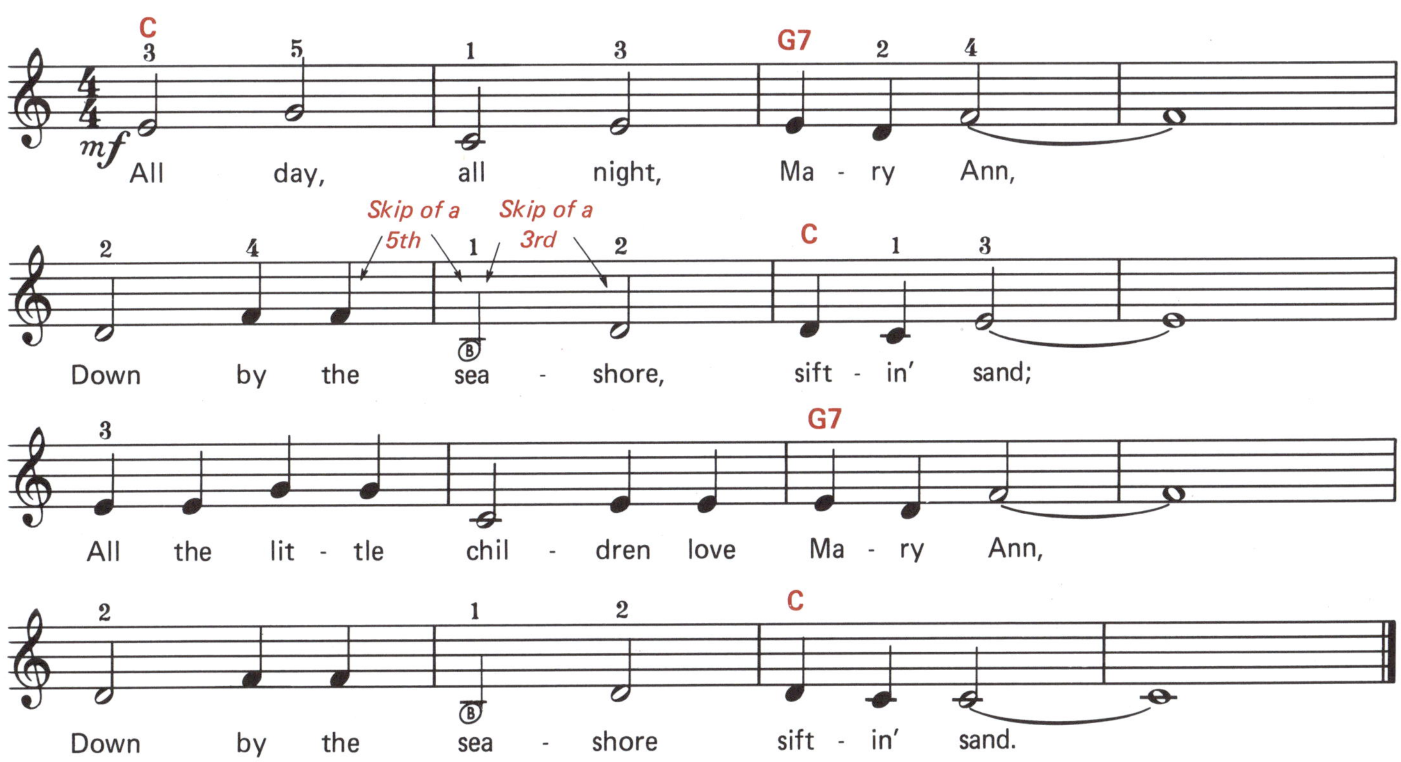

4. This piece is very effective with LATIN Rhythms. Try RHUMBA, SAMBA, OR BEGUINE.
5. Add VARIATION & DUET, if you have them. Use the ENDING button, if available.

About "Fingered Chords"

The "Fingered Chord" setting allows you to form your own three- and four-note LH chords just as you would play them on a piano, organ, synthesizer, or any keyboard instrument not equipped with automatic chords.

Knowing how to play "Fingered Chords" has other advantages:

1. Fingered Chords may be played the same on all makes and models of instruments. (This is not true of "Single Finger " chords.)
2. There are some chords that cannot be made on "Single Finger" setting. When you use Fingered Chords, you will be able to play any chord you see in popular sheet music.

When you use Fingered Chords, your instrument can still add all the features of the "Single Finger" setting, such as RHYTHMS, VARIATION, DUET, etc.

In *MARY ANN,* you used the following "Single Finger" chords: C MAJOR and G^7

These same chords are easily played as "Fingered Chords" without changing your LH position. By playing all Fingered Chords in the area between the two F's of the accompaniment section, you will be able to move smoothly from one chord to the next.

The C MAJOR CHORD (which consists of the notes C E G) will be played in the position: G C E.
The G^7 CHORD (G B D F) will be played with the D omitted: G B F.

Play the following chords with the LH.
Use **Auto:** ON "Fingered Chord." Do not press START or SYNCHRO. Listen to the sounds of these sustained chords, and practice changing from one to another.

C

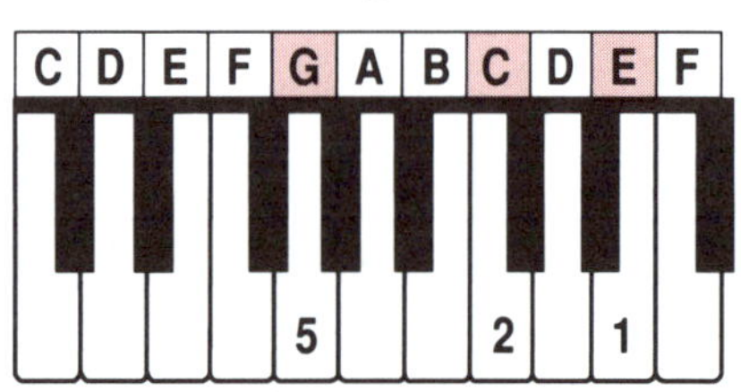

G^7

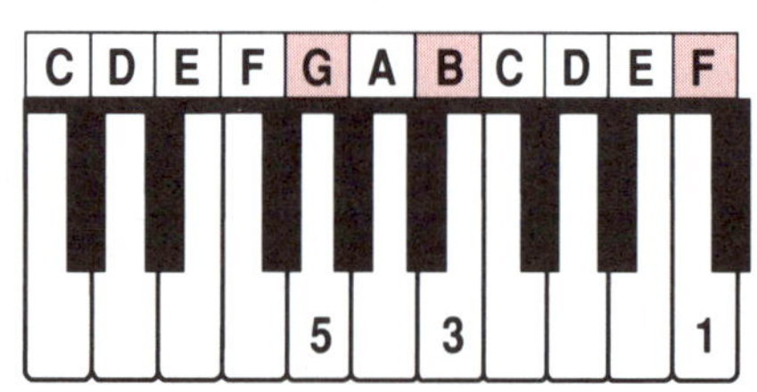

3. Practice the following with LH. Use **Auto:** ON "Fingered Chord." Do not press START or SYNCHRO.
4. Repeat, adding **Rhythm:** Slow MARCH or SWING. Press SYNCHRO and play. Just touch each chord and release it, counting "1-2-3-4" for each measure.

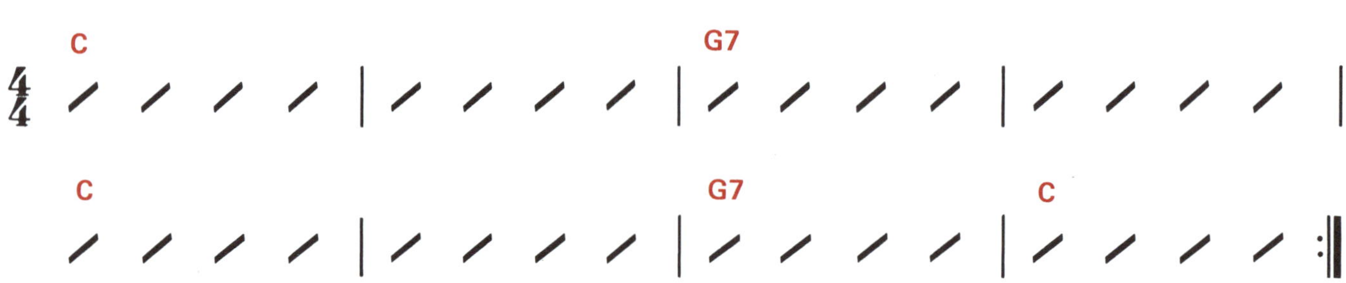

IMPORTANT! Play *MARY ANN,* using **Auto:** ON "Fingered Chords." Use Rhythms and Registers you have used before. Press SYNCHRO, then begin. Add any special effects you wish.

New Time Signature

3 means **3** beats to each measure.
4 means a **QUARTER NOTE** ♩ gets one beat.

Dotted Half Note

A **DOTTED HALF NOTE** gets 3 counts.
(2 counts for the half note,
plus 1 count for the dot!)

COUNT: "1 - 2 - 3"

Clap (or tap) the following rhythm.

Clap **ONCE** for each note, counting aloud.

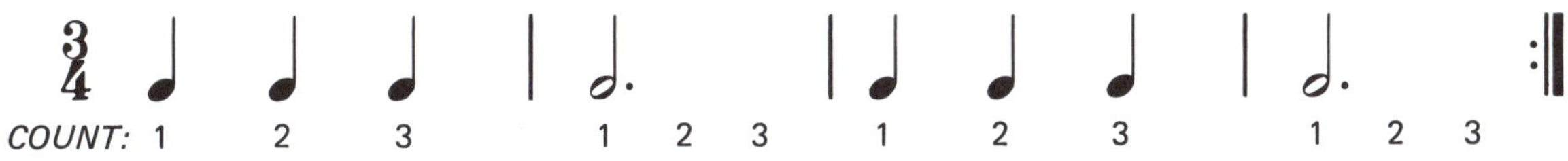

Set Auto Rhythm on WALTZ. Press START and let the instrument beat a few measures. Select a moderate, comfortable TEMPO. Clap or tap the above measures several times, counting "1-2-3" for each measure.

IMPORTANT! Always use WALTZ rhythm for music in $\frac{3}{4}$ time!

AN OLD-FASHIONED WALTZ

Auto: ON "Single Finger"
Rhythm: WALTZ

Register: PIANO, HARPSICHORD or MUSIC BOX
Sustain: ON

1. Play RH alone. Count aloud.
2. Add Rhythm: Use the same moderate tempo you used above. Count "1-2-3," then play RH again.
3. Add LH: Press SYNCHRO, then begin.
4. Play again, adding any effects you choose, such as DUET, VARIATION, ARPEGGIO, etc.

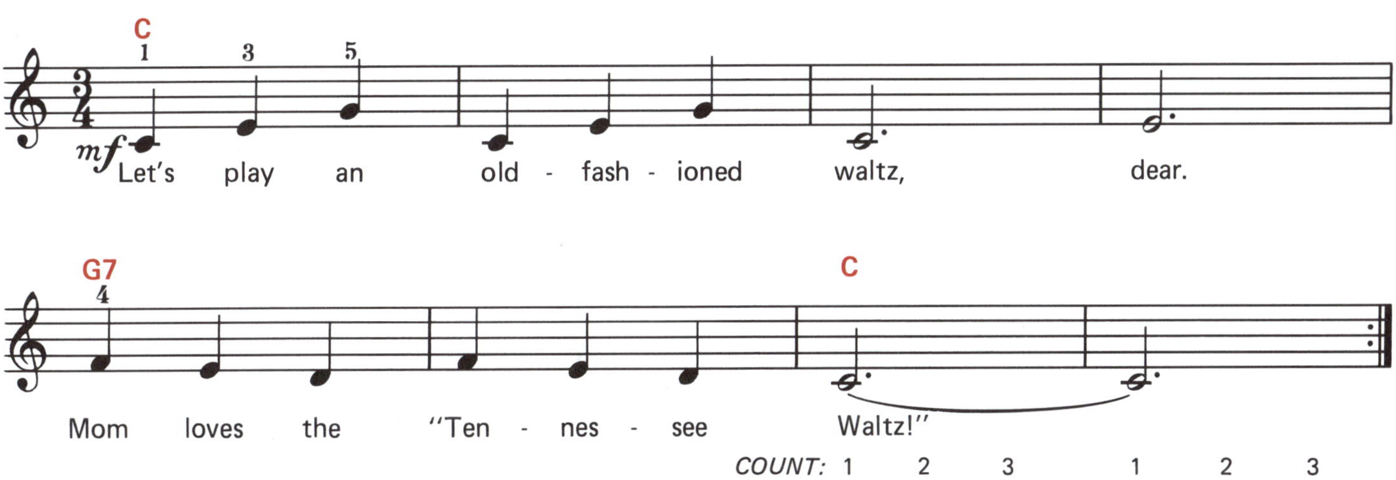

NOTE: You can make the melody stand out more clearly by turning the Chord volume and Rhythm volume DOWN, and turning the *Master* volume UP!

IMPORTANT! Play *OLD FASHIONED WALTZ* using **Auto:** ON "Fingered Chord."
Use the chord positions shown on page 30.

Slurs & Legato Playing

REVIEW: A **SLUR** is a curved line over or under notes on *different* lines or spaces.

SLURS mean play LEGATO (smoothly connected).

Slurs often divide the music into PHRASES.

A PHRASE is a musical thought or sentence.

DON'T BUY ME RIBBONS

Auto: ON "Single Finger"
Rhythm: Moderately slow WALTZ

Register: PIANO, VIBES, MUSIC BOX, or GUITAR
Sustain: ON

1. Play RH alone without Rhythm. Count aloud.
2. Add Rhythm: Press START. Adjust TEMPO. Count "1-2-3," then play RH again.
3. Add LH: Press SYNCHRO, then begin.

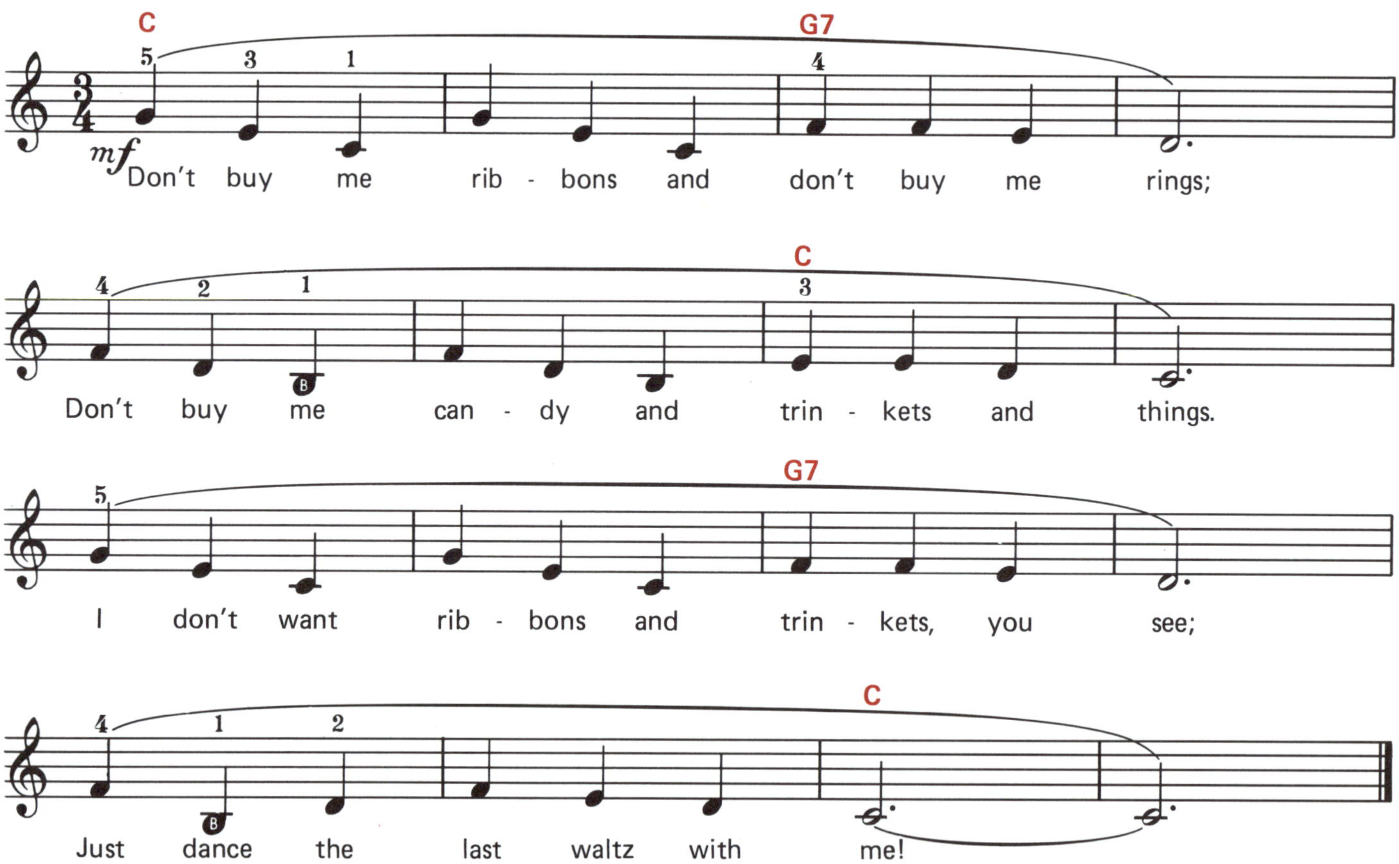

4. Play again. Add any other effects you wish, such as DUET, VARIATION, ARPEGGIO, VIBRATO, STEREO, REVERB, etc.

IMPORTANT! Play *DON'T BUY ME RIBBONS* using **Auto:** ON "Fingered Chord."
Use the following LH positions:

C

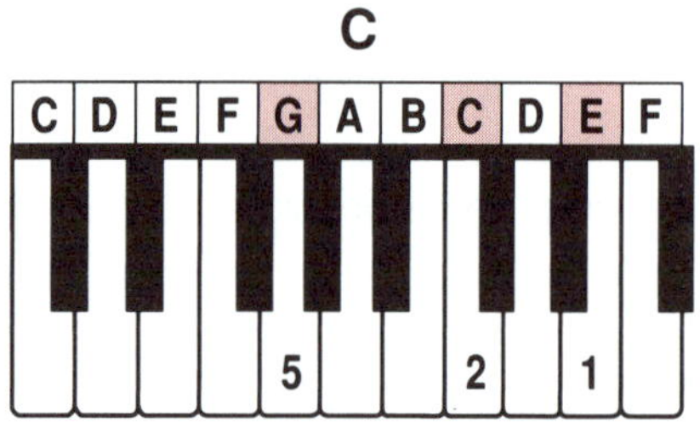

G^7

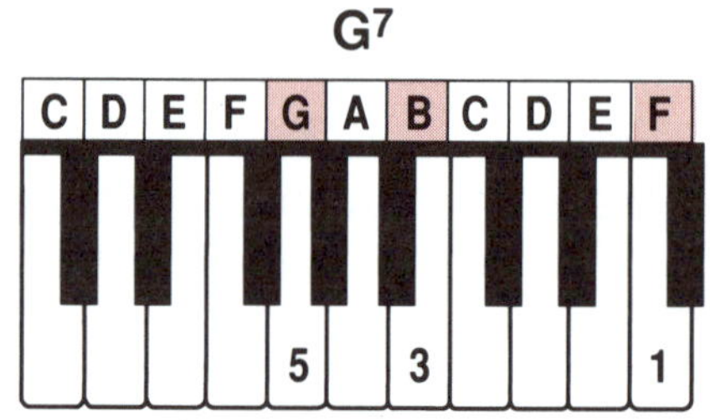

Rhythm Man

RESTS are signs of **SILENCE.**

This is a **QUARTER REST**
It means REST FOR THE VALUE OF A QUARTER NOTE.

Auto: ON "Single Finger"
Rhythm: Moderately slow MARCH

Register: ORGAN or TRUMPET
Sustain: OFF

1. Play the RH alone several times, without Rhythm. Count aloud.
2. Add Rhythm: Press START. Adjust TEMPO. Count "1-2-3-4," then play RH again.
3. Add LH: Press SYNCHRO, then begin. Listen to what the Auto Rhythm plays during the rests.

Play again, using COUNTRY or SWING Rhythm.
Add VARIATION & DUET, along with other available effects.

Play and Rest a While

This is a **HALF REST.**

It means REST FOR THE VALUE OF A HALF NOTE.

Auto: ON "Single Finger"
Rhythm: Moderately slow SWING or MARCH

Register: ORGAN or TRUMPET
Sustain: OFF

NOTE: Use steps 1, 2 and 3 shown in *RHYTHM MAN.* This procedure is excellent for learning any new song. Use it for the remaining pages of this book!

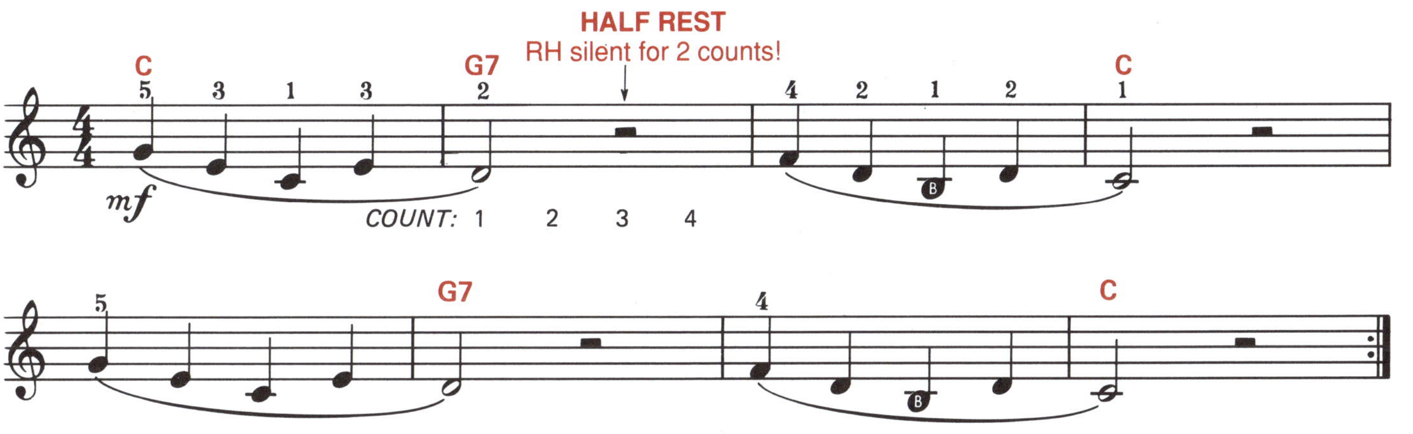

Play again with other Rhythms. Add VARIATION & DUET, if available.

IMPORTANT! Play *RHYTHM MAN* and *PLAY AND REST A WHILE* using **Auto**: ON "Fingered Chord."
Use the chord positions shown on page 32.

Beautiful Brown Eyes

Auto: ON "Single Finger"
Rhythm: Moderately fast WALTZ

Register: GUITAR or PIANO
Sustain: ON

1. Use steps 1, 2 and 3 shown in *RHYTHM MAN.*
2. Play again, adding VARIATION or ARPEGGIO, DUET and other effects.

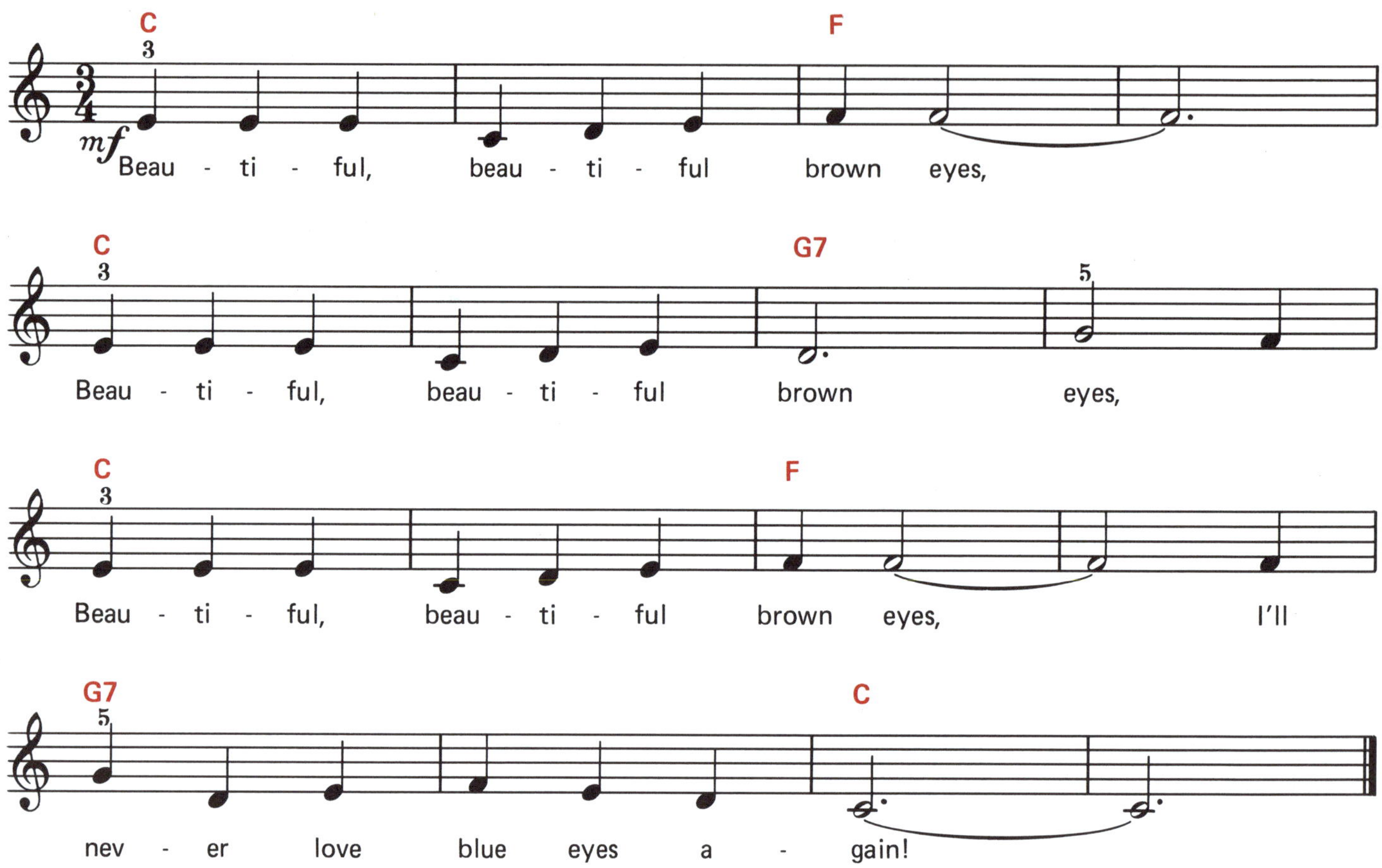

Introducing the F Major "Fingered Chord"

The F MAJOR CHORD (F A C) will be played in the position: A, C, F, with 4, 2, 1.

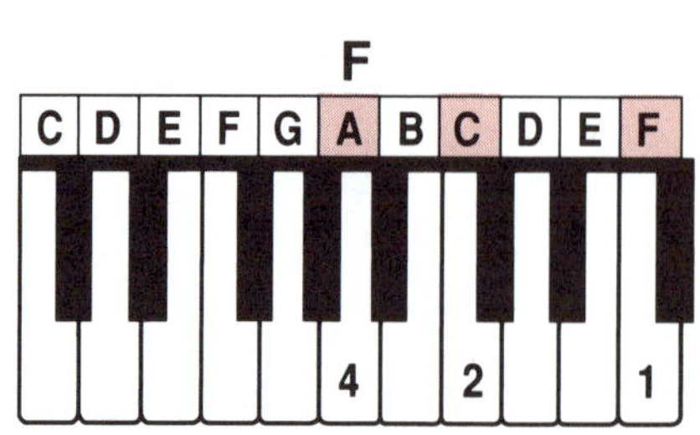

Play the F Major "Fingered Chord" shown above.
Use **Auto:** On "Fingered Chord." Do not press START or SYNCHRO. Listen to the sound of this sustained chord.

Left Hand Warm-Up

You have learned the following three "Fingered Chords":

C

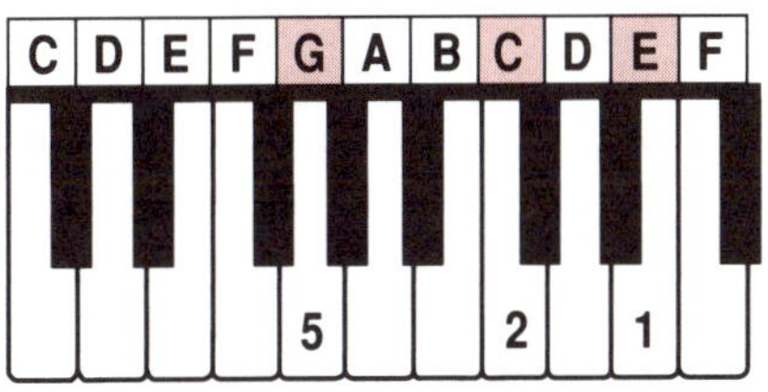

F

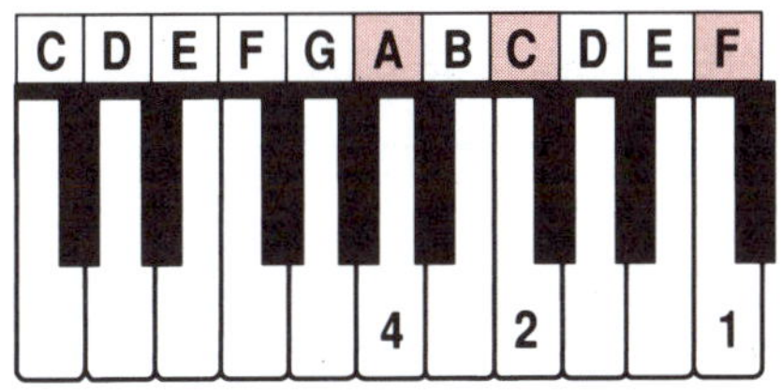

G7

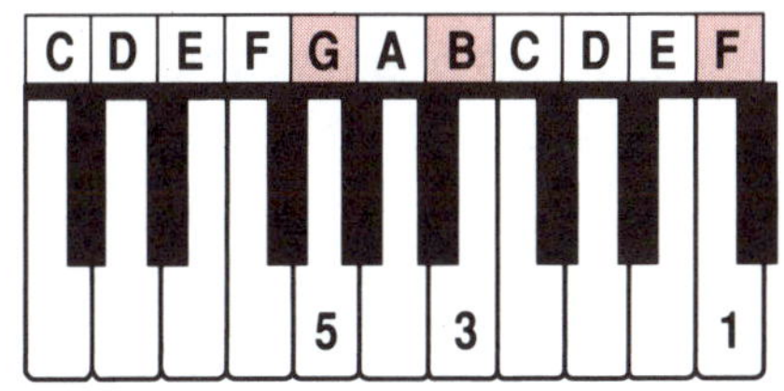

Play the following several times.
Use **Auto:** On "Fingered Chord" and **Rhythm:** Moderately slow WALTZ.

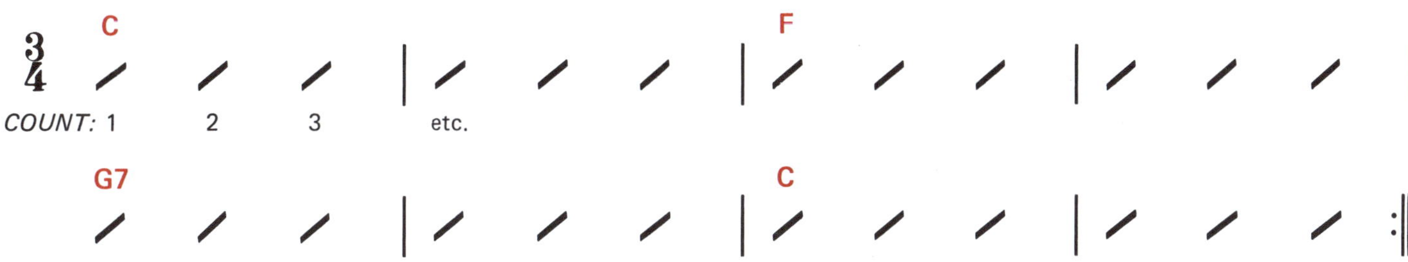

IMPORTANT: Play *BEAUTIFUL BROWN EYES* using **Auto:** On "Fingered Chord."
Use the chord positions shown above.

Duet Part for Beautiful Brown Eyes

For performance by the teacher or another student on the SAME KEYBOARD or a different one.
This part may be programmed into the keyboard memory (if available) or a sequencer.
The student can then play along as the duet part is played back.

When playing on the SAME KEYBOARD, play the duet part 8va (one octave higher).

*Play *p* if performed on a different keyboard.

INCOMPLETE MEASURE

Some pieces begin with an INCOMPLETE MEASURE. The first measure of this piece has only 3 counts. The missing count is found in the last measure! When you repeat the whole song, you will have one whole measure of 4 counts when you play the last measure plus the first measure.

The notes of an incomplete measure are sometimes called "PICK-UP" notes.

When the Saints Go Marching In

Auto: ON "Single Finger"
Rhythm: Slow MARCH, SWING or POP

Register: TRUMPET, CLARINET, SAX or TROMBONE
Sustain: OFF

1. Play RH alone. Count "2-3-4" on the "pick-up" notes. The next note is a WHOLE NOTE tied to a QUARTER NOTE. Hold it for 5 counts (count "1-2-3-4, 1").
2. When adding LH, press SYNCHRO, and play the first LH C exactly on the note above which the chord symbol appears. When you make the indicated repeat, the single count in the last measure added to the 3 counts of the first measure will make exactly one complete measure. The Rhythm will continue as you repeat, and there will be no need to play the first LH C again.

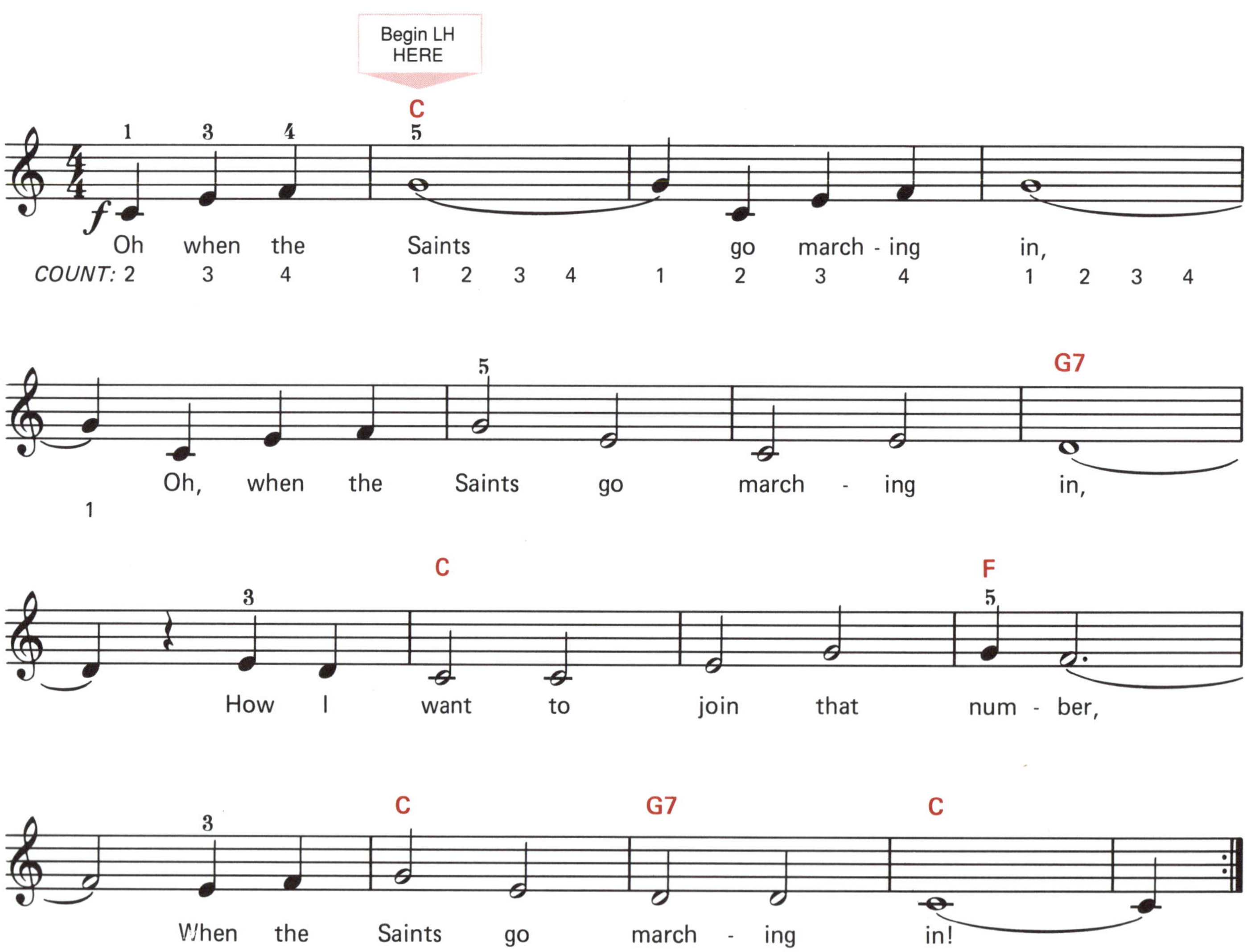

3. Play again. Add any other effects you choose, such as DUET, VARIATION, ARPEGGIOS, VIBRATO, STEREO, etc.

IMPORTANT: Play *WHEN THE SAINTS GO MARCHING IN* using **Auto:** ON "Fingered Chord."
Use the chord positions shown below.

C

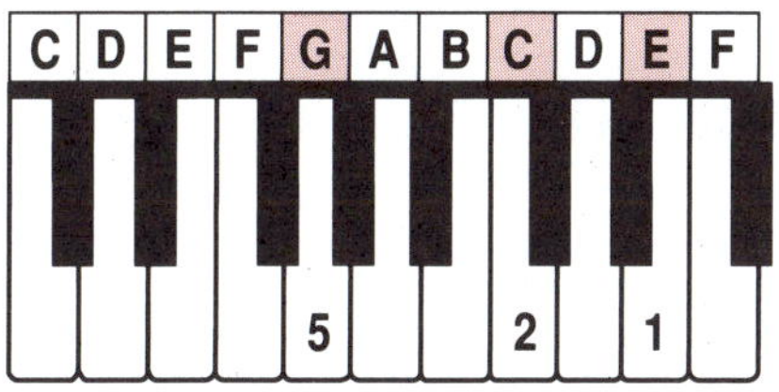

G^7

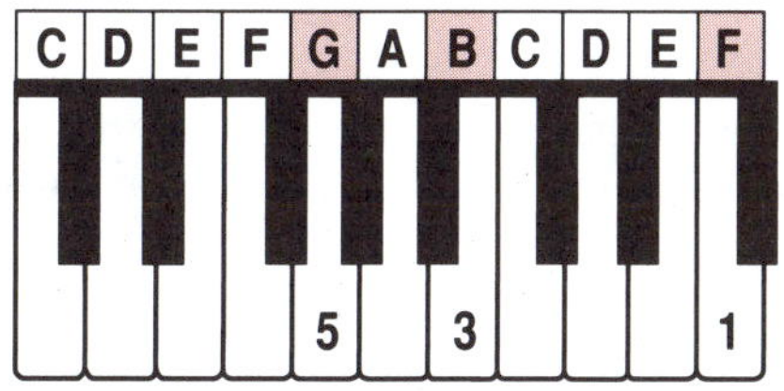

F

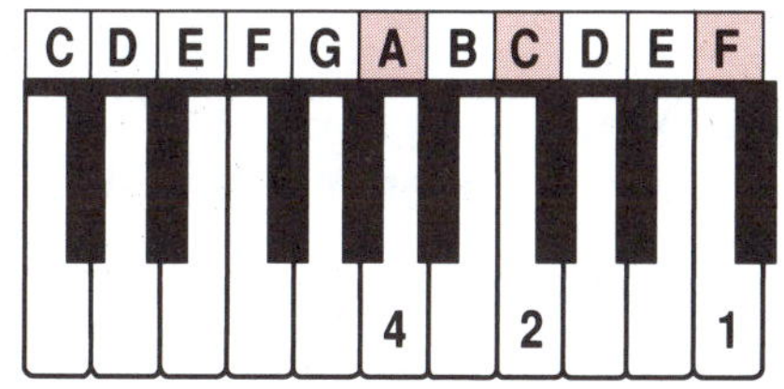

Duet Part for When the Saints Go Marching In

This part may be played by the teacher or another student on ANOTHER KEYBOARD.

It may be programmed into the memory of the SAME KEYBOARD, however, and the student can then play along as the duet part is played back.

*On some instruments, the programmed DUET PART will begin to play only when the first LH chord is played (see melody part on previous page). If this is true of your instrument, omit the small notes when programming the DUET PART.

The Peanut Song

This is a **WHOLE REST:** ▬

It means REST FOR THE VALUE OF A WHOLE NOTE or any WHOLE MEASURE.

Auto: ON "Single Finger"
Rhythm: Moderately fast SWING or COUNTRY

Register: ORGAN or TRUMPET
Sustain: OFF

1. Use the same steps listed on page 33 for learning *THE PEANUT SONG.*
2. Add any other effects you choose. Try different Registers, including PIANO and GUITAR with Sustain ON. Try other Rhythms, including SLOW ROCK, SHUFFLE and POP, if they are available.

3. Play *THE PEANUT SONG* using **Auto:** ON "Fingered Chord."

Introducing (A) for Right Hand

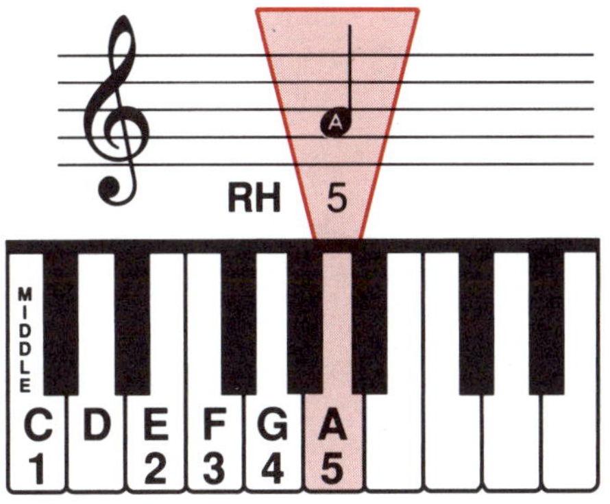

TO FIND A:
Place the RH in **C POSITION.** Leave 1 on C.
Shift all other fingers one white key to the right!

Play slowly. Say the note names as you play.

Auto: OFF
Rhythm: OFF

Register: PIANO
Sustain: ON

GRANDPA'S ROCKIN'!

Auto: ON "Single Finger"
Rhythm: Moderate Swing or Rock 'n' Roll

Register: PIANO, ORGAN, VIBES, or GUITAR
Sustain: ON

1. Use steps listed on page 33.
2. Use VARIATION & DUET, if available.

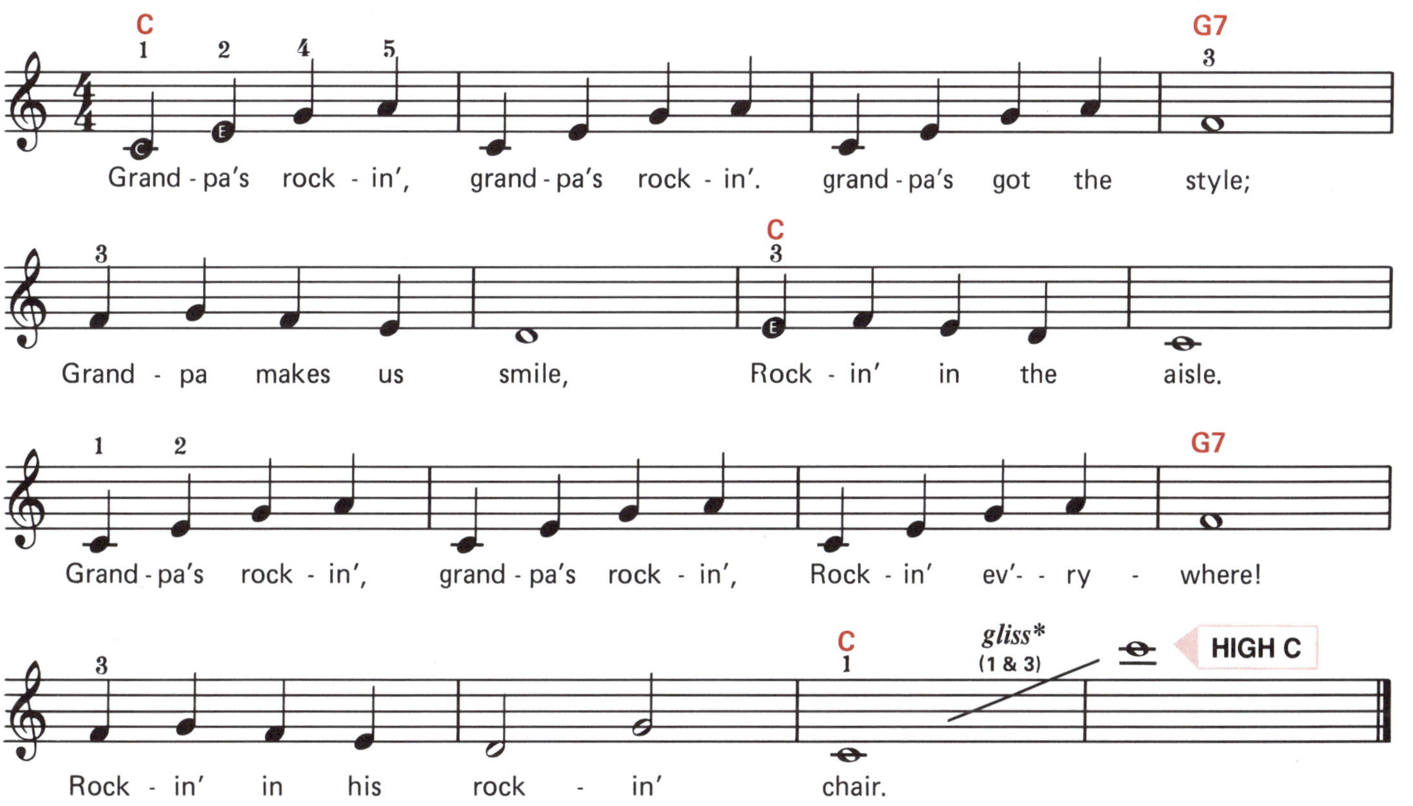

3. Play *GRANDPA'S ROCKIN'* using **Auto:** On "Fingered Chord."

* *GLISS* stands for *glissando,* which means "sliding." Using RH 1 & 3 together, slide over the keys, all the way up the keyboard to the highest key.

Right Hand G Position

Place the RH on the keyboard so the **1st FINGER** falls on the G above middle C.
Let the remaining four fingers fall naturally on the next four white keys.
Keep the fingers curved and relaxed.

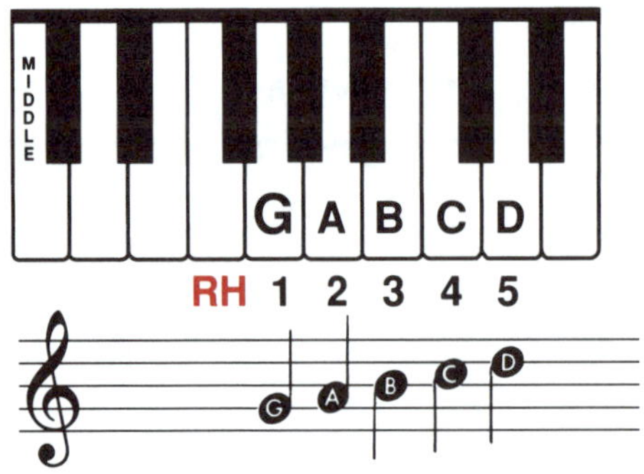

Auto: OFF **Rhythm:** OFF **Register:** PIANO **Sustain:** ON

Play and say the note names. Be sure to do this SEVERAL TIMES!

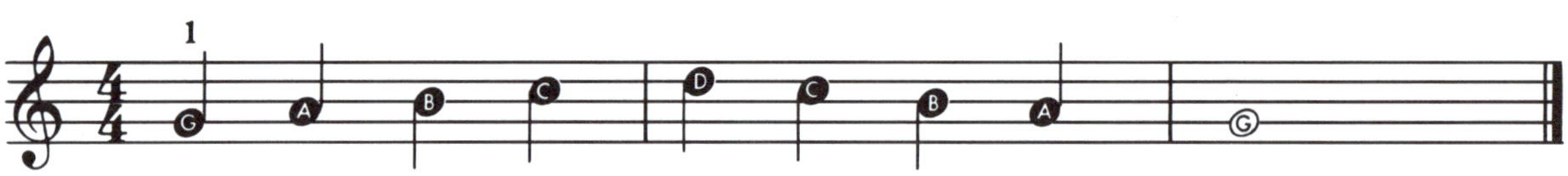

Intervals in G Position

Auto: OFF **Rhythm:** OFF **Register:** PIANO **Sustain:** ON

Say the name of each interval as you play.

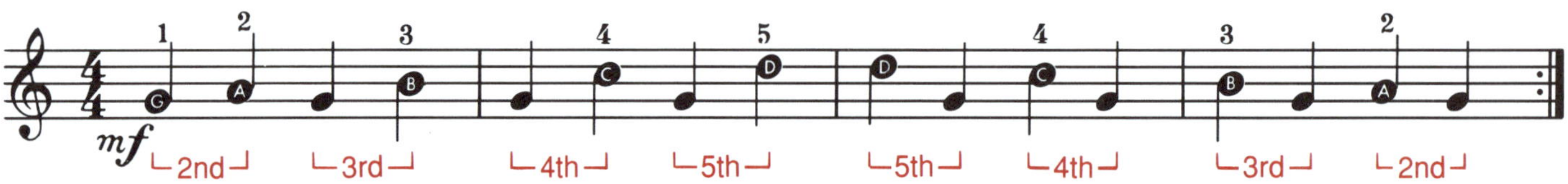

Note Reading Exercise

Say the name of each note as you play.

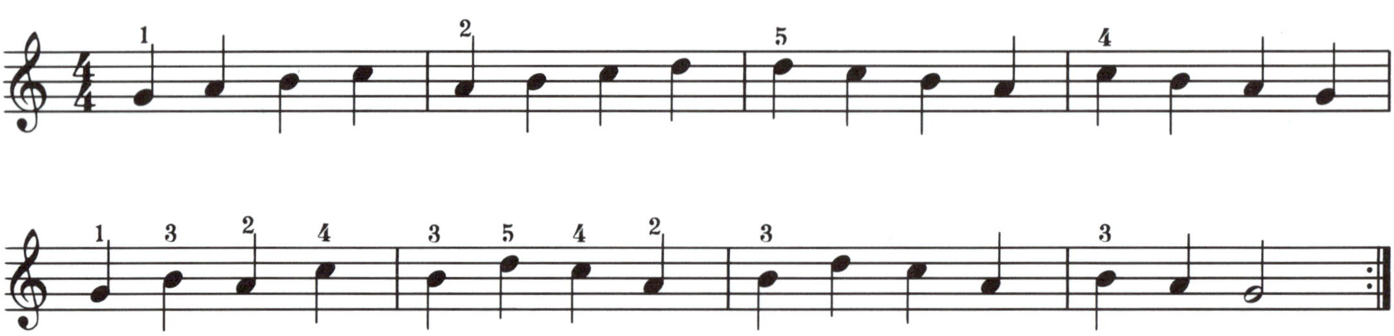

Try with various registers.

Left Hand G Position

NOTE: For the pieces in the following section of this book, the basic LH position remains unchanged (see page 18). The thumb will be playing D instead of F. Notice that the thumb falls naturally on the D.

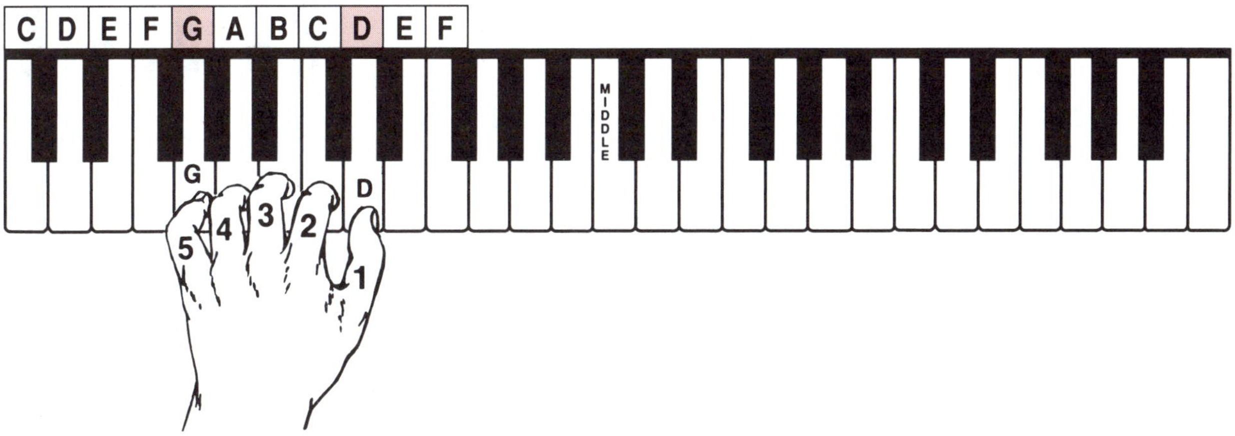

LOVE SOMEBODY!

G POSITION

f* – *p means 1st time ***f***, 2nd time ***p***.

Auto: ON "Single Finger"
Rhythm: Moderately fast SWING or COUNTRY

Register: PIANO or GUITAR
Sustain: ON

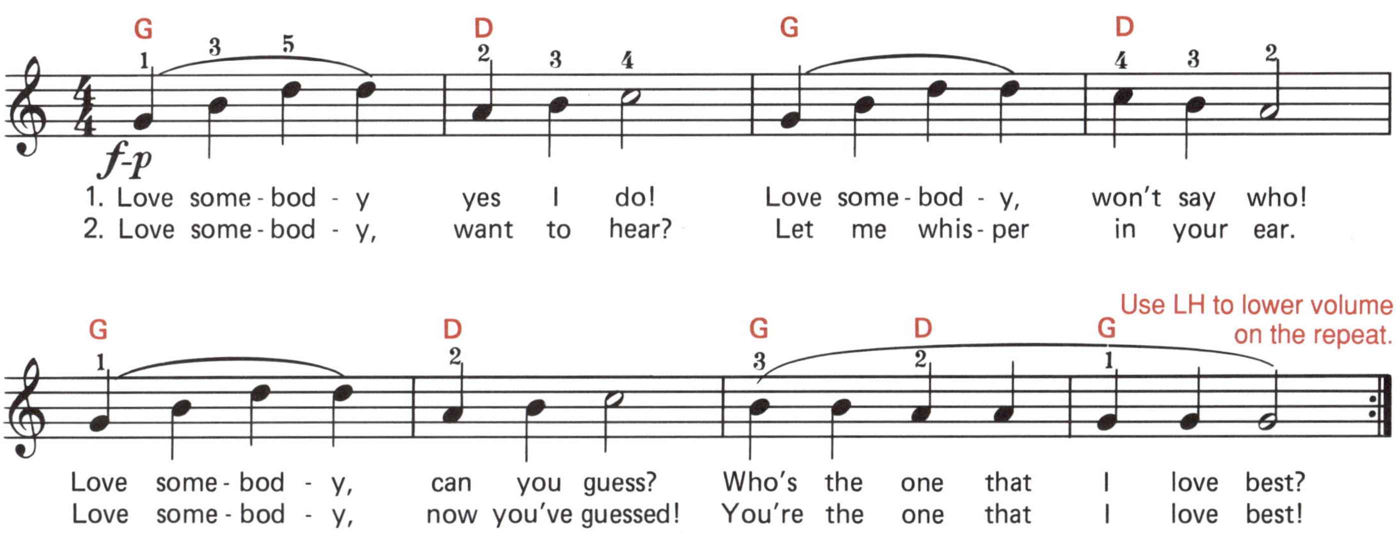

Play again. Add any other effects you wish, such as DUET, VARIATION, ARPEGGIO, VIBRATO, STEREO, REVERB, etc.*

*VIBRATO produces a fluctuation in the sound, similar to the natural vibrato of the voice, or that produced on a violin or guitar by an oscillation of the finger holding the string down.

STEREO causes the sound to be distributed between the right and left speakers to produce a stereophonic effect, providing an orchestra-like presence.

REVERB produces a slight echo effect, simulating the sound of an instrument played in a concert hall.

These features are not available on all instruments.

The "Single Finger" D^7 Chord

In this piece you will be using the "single finger" D^7 chord for the first time.

REMEMBER:

On CASIO and REALISTIC instruments, play the key-note (**D**) plus the next TWO WHITE KEYS to the right.

For D^7, play D, E & F. Use LH 3 2 1.
(Shift LH position two keys to the right.)

D7

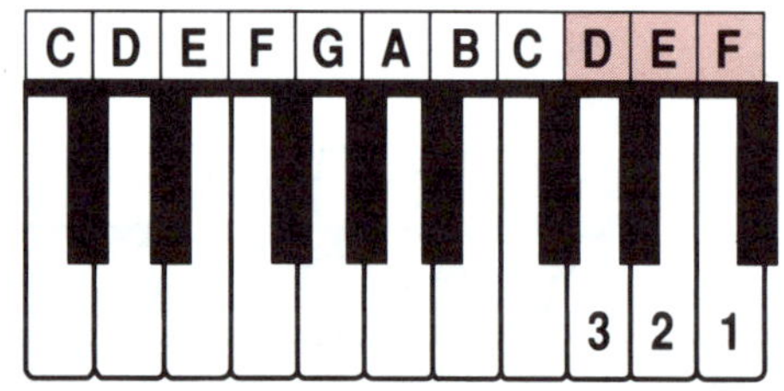

On YAMAHA, BALDWIN, and TECHNICS instruments, play the key-note (**D**) plus the NEXT WHITE KEY to the left.

For D^7, play C & D. Use LH 2 1.
(You will not need to change LH position.)

D7

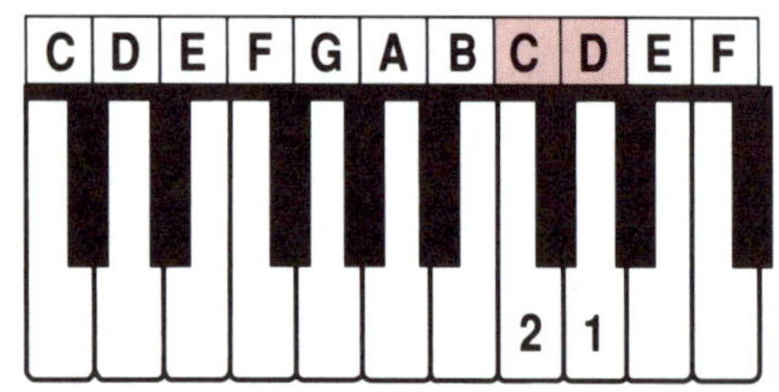

On LOWRY & new KAWAI keyboards, the D7 chord is made this way.

IMPORTANT! Play the D^7 chord using **Auto:** ON "Single Finger." Do not press START or SYNCHRO. Listen to the sound of the sustained chord.

A Friend Like You

G POSITION

Auto: ON "Single Finger"
Rhythm: Moderately slow COUNTRY, SWING or POP

Register: GUITAR, HAWAIIAN GUITAR, or TRUMPET
Sustain: OFF

This piece begins with an INCOMPLETE MEASURE of only 3 counts. The last measure has only 1 count. When you make the indicated repeat, you will have one whole measure of 4 counts when you play the last measure plus the first measure. The Rhythm will continue as you repeat, and there will be no need to touch the first LH G again.

Practice hands separately at first.

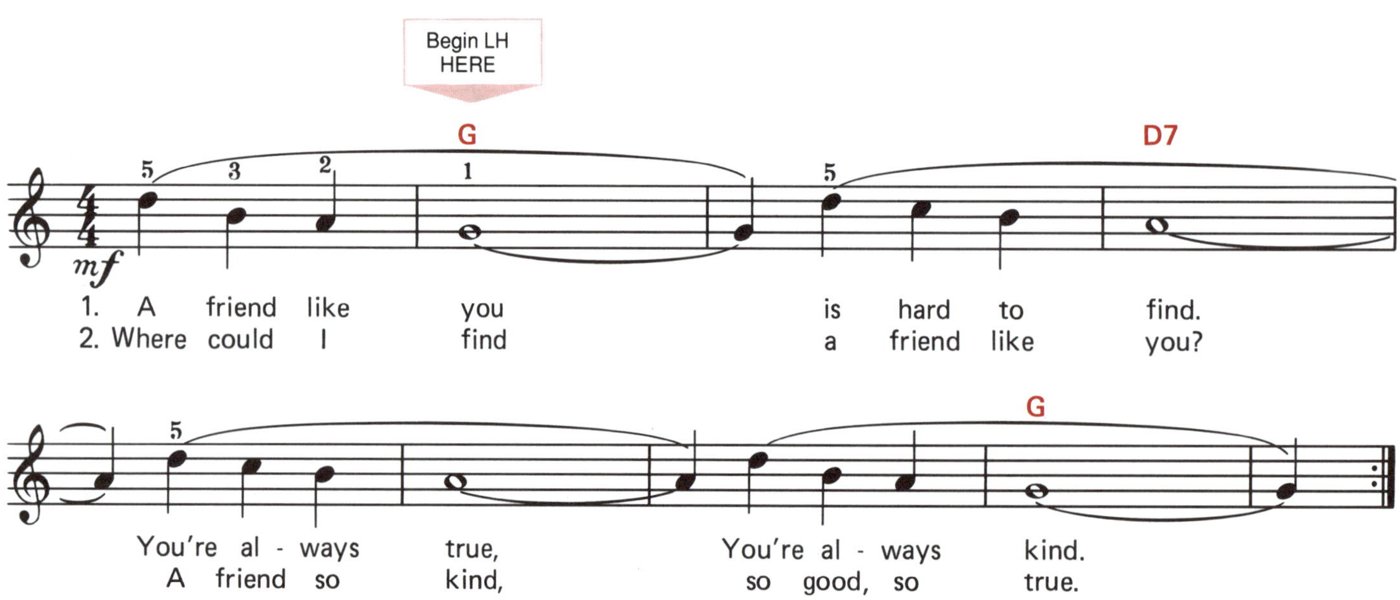

Play again, adding VARIATION and DUET, if available.

The Sharp Sign

The **SHARP SIGN** before a note means play the next key to the RIGHT, whether black or white!

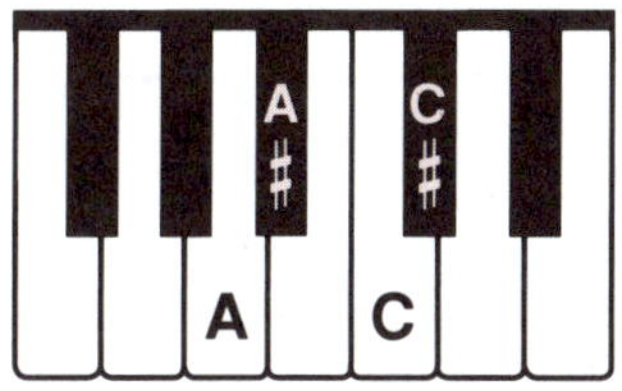

When a SHARP (♯) appears before a note, it applies to that note for the rest of the measure!

Circle the notes that are SHARP:

MONEY CAN'T BUY EV'RYTHING!
without Chords

Auto: OFF
Rhythm: Moderately fast SWING, COUNTRY or slow MARCH

Register: BANJO, PIANO or GUITAR
Sustain: ON

1. Practice slowly at first without Auto Rhythm, counting aloud. (Do not press START.)
2. Press START, adjust tempo, then play with Auto Rhythm.

G POSITION

Money Can't Buy Ev'rything!
with "Single Finger" Chords

This sign is called a **FERMATA.**

Hold the note under the FERMATA longer than its value.

A two-measure *introduction** and a three-measure *ending** have been added to this version. From the *introduction* you can get the feel of the tempo and rhythm by the time the RH melody begins to play. The *fermata,* mentioned above, will be used in the *ending.*

Auto: ON "Single Finger"
Rhythm: Moderately fast SWING, COUNTRY or slow MARCH

Register: BANJO, PIANO or GUITAR
Sustain: ON

1. Press SYNCHRO and play LH alone. Adjust tempo and begin again, if necessary. In the very last measure play LH G again and HOLD IT. At the same time, press the STOP button with the RH. Let the sound of the final chord continue as long as you wish.
2. Play with BOTH hands. Press SYNCHRO and begin with LH. Add RH after counting "1-2-3-4" twice for the two-measure intro.
3. Play again, adding VARIATION, and DUET, if available.

* If your instrument has *intro* and *ending* buttons, you may wish to use them here.
Please check your OWNER'S MANUAL.

The "Fingered" G Major & D^7 Chords

The Fingered G CHORD consists of the notes G, B, D.

The Fingered D^7 CHORD consists of the notes D, F♯, A, C. For convenience in playing, the A is omitted, and the chord is played in this position: F♯ C D.

G

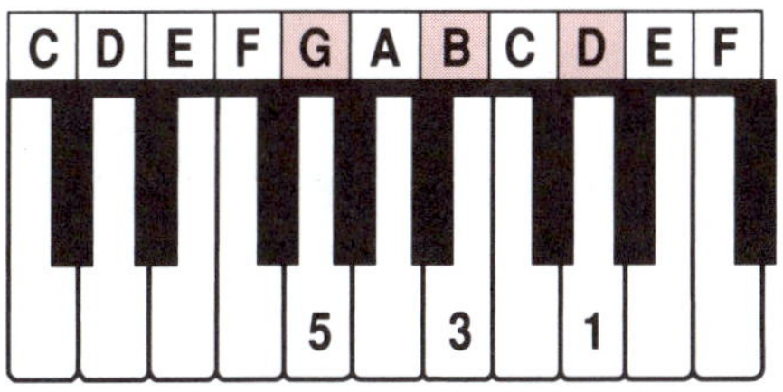

D^7

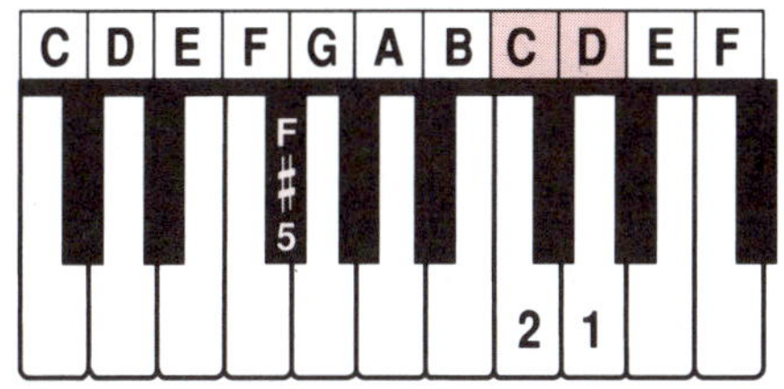

Practice playing the Fingered G MAJOR and D^7 CHORDS. Listen to the sounds!
Use **Auto:** ON "Fingered Chord." Do not press START or SYNCHRO. Practice changing from one chord to the other.

1. Practice the following with LH. Use **Auto:** ON "Fingered Chord." Do not press START or SYNCHRO. HOLD EACH CHORD down for two full measures!
2. Repeat, adding **Rhythm:** Moderately fast SWING or slow MARCH. Press SYNCHRO and begin. Just touch each chord and release it, counting "1-2-3-4" for each measure.

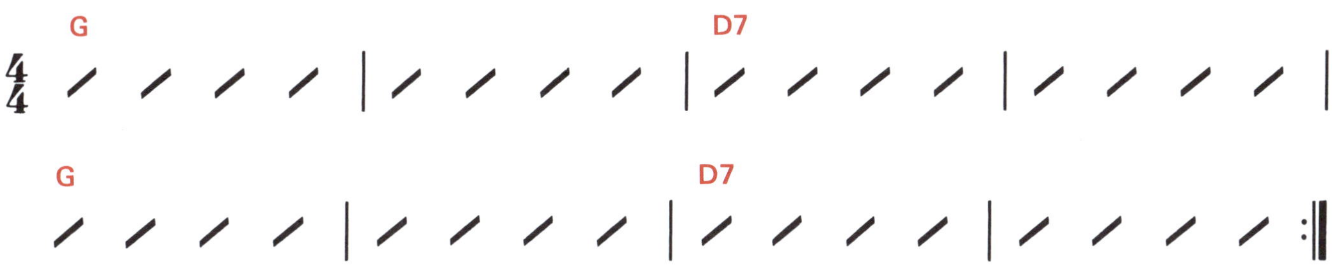

The Donkey

Auto: ON "Fingered Chord" **Register:** PIANO **Sustain:** ON

Play with sustained chords, then with **Rhythm:** Moderately fast SWING, COUNTRY or POP.

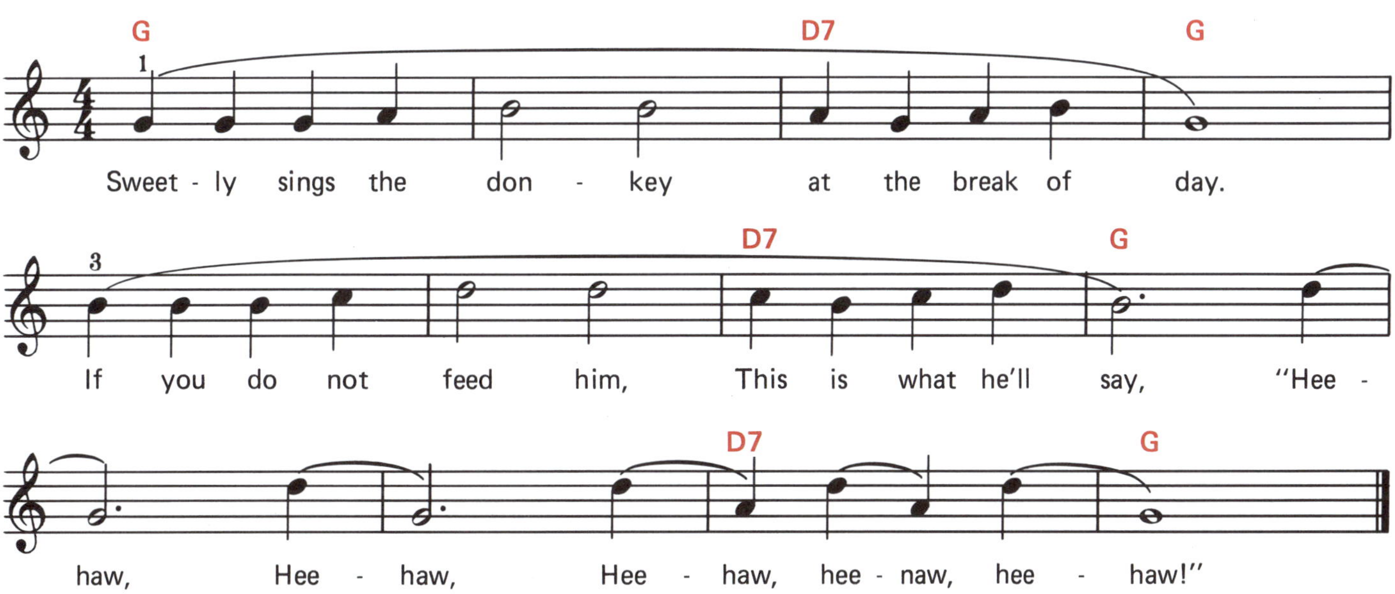

IMPORTANT! Play *MONEY CAN'T BUY EV'RYTHING!* (page 44) again.
Use **Auto:** ON "Fingered Chord."

Jingle Bells
(C Position and "Single Finger" Chord Review)

This piece is fun to play any time of the year.
Here it is arranged to review all of the "Single Finger" chords you have used so far.

Auto: ON "Single Finger"
Rhythm: Moderately fast SWING, or slow MARCH

Register: PIANO, VIBES, MUSIC BOX or BELLS
Sustain: OFF

1. Play RH several times alone.
2. Add LH. Press SYNCHRO and begin. Play the repeat with a different register, if you wish.
3. Add DUET, VARIATION and any other effects you choose.

Reviewing the "Fingered Chords"

IMPORTANT! Play JINGLE BELLS, using **Auto:** ON "Fingered Chord." Use the chord positions shown below.

C

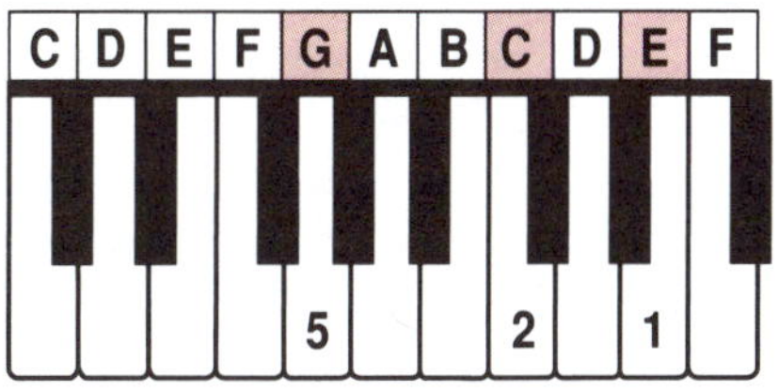

F

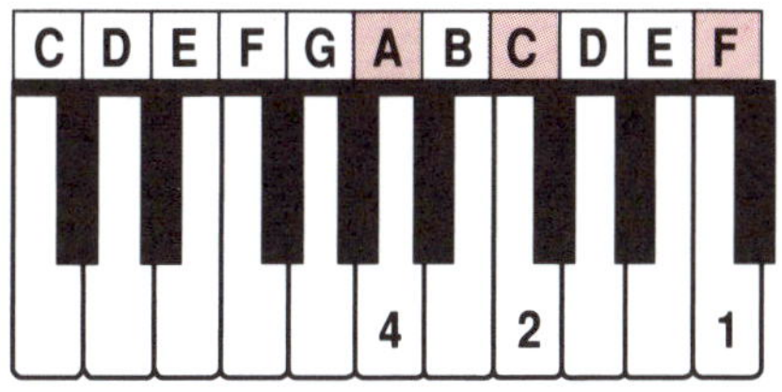

D7

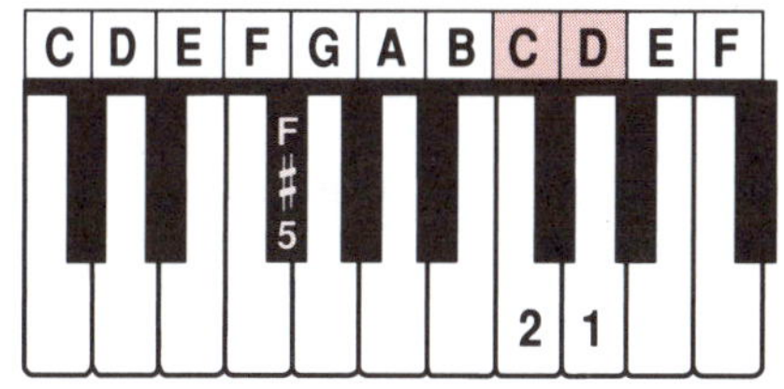

G

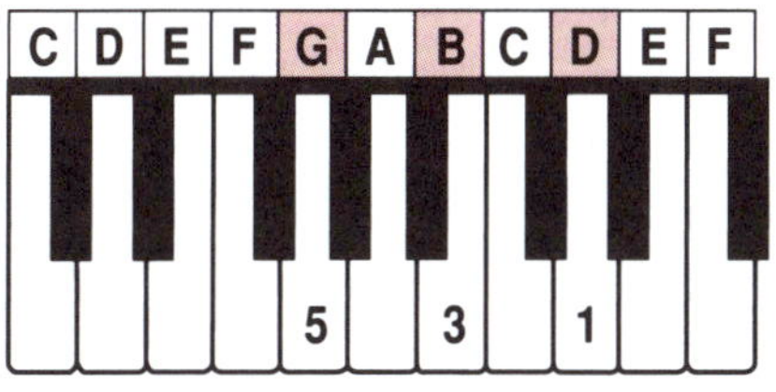

G7

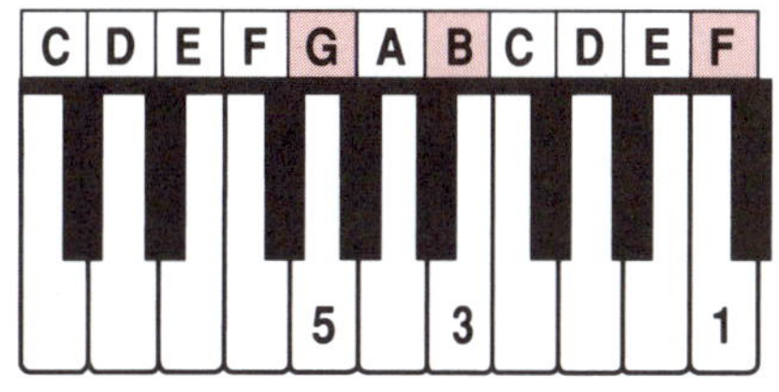

Duet Part for JINGLE BELLS

This part may be played by the teacher or another student on the SAME KEYBOARD, or it may be programmed into the keyboard memory or a sequencer, if available. The student can then play along as the duet is played back.

Use an appropriate register, such as MUSIC BOX, BELLS, VIBES or PIANO.

Certificate of Promotion

THIS CERTIFIES THAT

HAS SUCCESSFULLY COMPLETED **Lesson Book 1** OF

Alfred's Basic Chord Approach to Electronic Keyboards COURSE

AND IS HEREBY PROMOTED TO **Lesson Book 2.**

Alfred Publishing Co., Inc.

Morty Manus

Morty Manus, President